JOHN
WOOLMAN

☆

The GREAT AMERICAN THINKERS *Series*

JOHN WOOLMAN:
The Mind of the Quaker Saint

Edwin H. Cady, Ph.D.
Rudy Professor of English
Indiana University

☆

SERIES EDITORS
Arthur W. Brown, Ph.D.
President, Adelphi University; and

Thomas S. Knight, Ph.D.
Professor and Chairman of the
Department of Philosophy, Adelphi University

WASHINGTON SQUARE PRESS, INC. • NEW YORK • 1966

FOR ELIZABETH

ACKNOWLEDGMENTS

Anyone who works with Woolman must immediately fall in debt to the works of Amelia Mott Gummere and Janet Whitney; and, as I have tried variously to indicate, I have done so. One also inevitably owes much to the great standard histories of Braithwaite (as edited by Cadbury) and Rufus Jones. But it was with delight and immense (if not inevitably correct) profit that I discovered the recent work of a brilliant group of Quaker and Pennsylvania historians. For me they have invaluably backlighted Woolman's cultural context.

Their dean is perhaps Frederick B. Tolles: *Meeting House and Counting House: The Quaker Merchants of Colonial Philadelphia, 1682–1763; James Logan and the Culture of Provincial America; Quakers and the Atlantic Culture.* But they include also Theodore Thayer, *Israel Pemberton, King of the Quakers;* Thomas E. Drake, *Quakers and Slavery in America;* Howard Brinton, esp. *Friends for 300 Years;* and Robert L. D. Davidson, *War Comes to Quaker Pennsylvania, 1682–1756.* The most recent, Sydney V. James, *A People Among Peoples: Quaker Benevolence in Eighteenth-Century America,* both synthesizes effectively and pioneers anew in its own way.

I am also inevitably and gladly indebted to libraries and their staffs—to the Friends Historical Library, Swarthmore College; to the Historical Society of Pennsylvania, the Library Company of Phila-delphia, and the American Philosophical Society. Charles Boewe and Whitfield J. Bell smoothed my way, and Miss Dorothy Harris went generously far beyond the call of duty to help me find what I needed. The staff and other resources of my own Indiana University Library were as always cheer-fully helpful.

Frank M. Davidson, William A. Eddy, Jr., Arthur S. Lloyd, Jack Lunn Mowers, David E. Smith, and William E. Wilson all read the manuscript. Pro-fessor Henry J. Cadbury was kind enough to point out certain errors in the first edition. The book is doubtless much the better for their often shrewd suggestions and the worse for suggestions stub-bornly ignored. Work in research and writing was generously supported by the Graduate School of Indiana University, John W. Ashton, Vice Presi-dent and Dean. As always, the work, like the author, owes more than could be said to Norma W. Cady.

CONTENTS

"In one particular respect the colonial Quakers made a very important contribution to religion—they produced saints, and these saints were and remain the finest and most fragrant bloom of American Quakerism. . . . invincibly fixed in purpose, genuinely heroic, ready for great deeds, possessed of infinite confidence in God, and withal tender in love and humility . . . they were triumphantly beautiful spirits, . . . and the beautiful life in the long run is dynamic and does inherit the earth.*

---

* "John Woolman is the consummate flower of the type I have in mind."

—Rufus Jones, *The Quakers in the American Colonies,* 1911

INTROIT

John Woolman, who died in 1772, was the soul of kindness, of quiet humility, of gentle Christian charity. Nevertheless he stands at this moment in unique and terrible judgment upon the United States of America. Wholly American, he did not live to see his country formed politically. Yet he lived and wrote to form its necessary conscience. More important, his moral imagination, vital after two centuries, invites us from the pages of his *Journal* and essays to create the conscience necessary to the health of the world as well as the nation of our times.

The roster of American saints is short and the public memory of their names shorter still. We have rightly felt that, on the whole, the national morality was best in the keeping of simple, unsung average men, not in any spiritual elite. But just now history if not God seems to demand a creative response from the American conscience which cannot remain inchoate. Within and without our borders the three most fateful American problems concern money, race, and power. Woolman speaks intimately, profoundly to our condition with regard to all three. He is a genuine American saint. We sorely need to hear his voice and feel the power of his aesthetic as well as his moral imagination.

Chapter I

SOME INDIANS AND A TRUE BELIEVER

While I was a little boy, once as I went to a neighbor's house I saw, on the way, a Robin sitting on her nest. And as I came near she went off, but, having young ones, flew about and with many cries expressed her Concern for them. I stood and threw stones at her till, one striking her, she fell down dead. At first I was pleased with the Exploit, but after a few minutes was seized with Horror—as having in a sportive way killed an Innocent Creature while she was careful of her young.

I beheld her lying dead, and thought those young ones for which she was so careful must now perish for want of their dam to nourish them. And after some painful considerations on the subject, I climbed up the tree, took all the young birds, and killed them supposing that better than to leave them to pine away and die miserably; and believed, in this case, that scripture proverb was fulfilled, "The tender mercies of the wicked are Cruel." I then went on my errand, but, for some hours could think of little else. . . .

Thus He whose tender Mercies are over all his works, hath placed that in the Human mind

which incites to exercise goodness towards
every living creature. . . .

John Woolman's credentials to historical importance and present relevance are impeccable. They
rise from his service to the cause of human freedom
and dignity, from the limpid beauty of the *Journal,*
which is his work of art and testament, and from
the vital appeal of his personal saintliness presented
through the *Journal.*

As to the importance and relevance of Woolman's
service to mankind we should almost all agree
readily. As Nathan Glazer says:

There is probably nothing more shameful in
the history of American religion than its complete abdication from any effort to help the
slaves—it acted only when asked by the slave-
masters, who thought religion might help keep
the slaves docile. . . . in the society fashioned
here in the United States, nothing was left to
prevent a cruelly logical reduction of the African to a piece of mere property.[1]

But Woolman is a shining contradiction to those
dreadful truths. It was he who turned the Religious
Society of Friends against slavery. His sharp vision
and compassion persuaded the Quakers to free their
slaves and thereafter take what responsibility they
could for them. He set the Friends as the corner-
stone of the American libertarian conscience. It is
also true that the reasons, religious and humane,
for Negro equality and human dignity upon which
Woolman patterned his testimonies for the slave

---

[1] S. M. Elkins, *Slavery* (New York: Universal Library, 1963):
Introduction by Nathan Glazer, p. xii.

[2]

remain fundamental to our national civil rights struggle and to our international racial problems in the immediate present. Finally, there is widespread agreement as to the force and beauty of Woolman's *Journal*. It is not only an American but a sort of international classic.

But then what of Woolman's saintliness? Are we not more than a little queasy about saints? They fall discomfortingly into a category we have been led of late to label "The True Believer."

This is not a place to examine at length Mr. Eric Hoffer's often brilliant, often exasperating book with its confessedly provocative half-truths, with its dogmatic worldly wisdom, Franklinian but naïve because it never achieves the elegance, complexity, or humility of Benjamin Franklin's final, self-reflexive irony. Subtitled "Thoughts on the Nature of Mass Movements," *The True Believer* frequently uses its avowed subject as a stalking horse from behind which to strike at belief in anything beyond that which a "gentle cynic" might find "real." The implication presses hard that the saint as true believer must be the same as the fanatic— a "spoiled" soul, frustrated and psychically suicidal, aiming at ruin, chaos, and agony, paradoxically at once a totalitarian fiend and the only agency history knows for "practical and desirable changes, such as the renovation of stagnant societies."

Let us agree at once with long-standing tradition that John Woolman is a saint—surely, in the pre-ironic sense of the phrase, a true believer. And to come to know him, first let us see him not as a triumphant libertarian but as he failed in a fascinating gesture of outreach toward a people doomed to historic tragedy—the Indians of Appalachian Pennsylvania in the eighteenth century. Perhaps thus we may see him first in a context like the contexts familiar to our age.

I

Two hundred years ago, asleep amid the fresh spring air of the night of June 5, 1763, John Woolman was wakened in his modest home by a summons from the local tavern in Mount Holly, N. J. There sat two earnest Quakers with a warning both friendly and well-informed. They could not know that in April the tragic Pontiac had launched the "conspiracy" which would forever determine the course of Indian-white relations in what was to be the United States. They did know, from a sensitive and expensive Quaker Indian intelligence system, that war parties and signs of bloody stirrings on the frontier were threatening still another irruption of horror from the wilderness onto the "back parts" of Pennsylvania. And they had come solemnly, but with undecorous haste past Quaker bedtime, to intercept John Woolman before he could set out next daybreak to visit certain wilderness Indians— the Delawares of Wyalusing, trembling on the thresholds of Christianity and European agrarian civilization.

Anybody but John Woolman, as he walked home to tell his "deeply concerned" wife the news, would have been impressed by the prestige of the messengers' concern for his well-being. They appear to have been Israel Pemberton, the uncrowned "King of the Quakers," and his brother John, both of Philadelphia. In all characteristics save one, the Pembertons were the antithesis of Woolman. They were of the city, sophisticated, and its party; he of the country, simple. They were rich, Israel in particular having not only inherited wealth but compounded it in mercantile operations not free from taints of smuggling, of dealing in the sinews of war, even of trafficking with the enemies of England's king, to whom he was subject. Woolman, a typical radical Quaker, had fought to free himself from every taint. He had deliberately gone out of business to ensure that worldly preoccupations should not usurp his spirituality. His life was given to worship in prayer and work, to pursuit of the inner assurance of the guidance of the will of God, and to effort as absolute as he could make it—fervently emotional, delicately sensitive to his own as well as other men's psyches, yet rigidly determined—to do that will.

The Pembertons were by temperament and practice organization men. They were deep in the politics of the colony, using and being used by Benjamin Franklin in their joint battles with the ex-Quaker Proprietors, weaving webs round the Governor. They were groping, in a challenging complex of cultural change, for an adequate creative response. Prosperity, frontier opportunism, and human frailty had broken up William Penn's "Holy Experiment," as all American utopian ventures have been dispelled. After a golden generation in flower, the resultant compromised Quaker culture had become threatened by the practical extinction which would at length be its fate. Not just materialism but ordinary cultivated worldliness drew figures and families like those of James Logan and other "Quaker grandees" out of the fold. Immigration, the crescent complexity of numbers and enterprise and civilization, and finally imperial war had repeatedly convulsed and at length extinguished Quaker political control over their Commonwealth.

Like the Mathers before them in post-theocratic New England, the Pembertons in post-Quakerly Pennsylvania led a movement to redeem the past in the present. The problem was twofold: internal and external. Internally they had not only to find means to order and consolidate by discipline the Religious Society and the culture of the Quakers; they also had to find objectives and methods adequate to a deep, fervent religious tradition. Externally they had to find oneness of action, points of contact, paths to acceptance, influence, prestige, and self-respect in the new society for the Quakers.

In the Friendly Commonwealth which succeeded the "Holy Experiment," the world had turned upside down. A "come-outer" radical sect, given to "enthusiasm," to prophetic evangelization, and to mysticism at subofficial levels of English society, had in Pennsylvania experienced, creatively but inadequately, the hazards of power. Now the world turned upside down again, and a culture neither obscurely subcultural nor any longer dominant on its own soil had to seek its fate in fecund, provincial America. Rich, well-connected, and able, the Pembertons might have made a profitable peace with the new powers. Instead they headed the essential struggle for Quaker survival. With money and imagination, with diplomacy, acuity, and energy, they devoted themselves to finding levers for the Quaker response. To none of these did they give more than to the Friendly Association for Regaining and Preserving Peace with the Indians by Pacific Measures.

And those, in brief, were the reasons why, after strenuous religious searchings had convinced John Woolman that he must nevertheless go on his journey, the Pembertons rode out with him on the morning of June 6, 1763—Israel as far as Woolman's

rendezvous with his Indian guides, John all the
way to Easton to see him launched into the forest.
Approaching on the whole from widely variant
points of vantage, Woolman and the Pembertons
were devoted to the same objects: the preservation
of Quaker culture, the revitalization of the Religious
Society of Friends, and the service of God.

II

Though Woolman's fascinating *Journal* account
gives small hint of the fact, it was no ordinary group
of Indians he was going to visit at Wyalusing. Almost heartbreakingly late in time—indeed, though
no one could know it for the moment, just after the
stroke of a historically fateful midnight—the Wyalusing Indians had become a phenomenon long
awaited and earnestly prayed for. They were a
community of Indians voluntarily seeking Christianity and civilization.

From the beginning of European time in the
Americas, plunder and the Gospel had competed
unequally for the Indian—and for the mind of the
white man as he considered the red. In Pennsylvania
no jewel in the crown of the "Holy Experiment"
sparkled so brightly as the Quaker success in
establishing good will, good faith, and enduring
peace with the Delawares of Penn's colony and
West New Jersey. Yet, while the Friends achieved
uniquely peace and justice, they succeeded no
better than Catholic or Calvinist in winning the
Indian to Christ or to agrarian culture.

Roy Harvey Pearce in his definitive study of
white America's ideas about the Indian ascribes this
failure to intellectual deficiencies:

Quakers travelled widely among Indians,
worked hard, but bothered themselves not at
all with theorizing, with constructing complex
systems for converting the savage heathen into
the civilized Christian. They could believe in
cultural complexity no more than ... in political complexity. They could offer the Indians
not ritual and dogma, but Love. Hence ...
they finished where they had begun, with a
simple faith in the saving awareness of the
divine principle in all men. Meantime, the Indians on the frontiers of Pennsylvania were
destroyed by that very cultural and political
complexity in which the Quakers could not
believe.[2]

There is, however, no doubt about the real human
complexity of the situation as faced by Woolman
or a Pemberton in 1763. Pennsylvania's heritage of
good faith and good will with the Delawares had
been compromised in 1732 by the colony's agreement with the Iroquois League, mythic feudatory
lords of the Delawares, and exhausted by the corrupt Walking Purchase of 1737. After the shattering
defeat of Braddock in 1755, the Pennsylvania
frontiers for the first time experienced the agonies
and terrors of Indian warfare. And their own Delawares had taken a leading part, to the permanent
destruction of the Quaker heritage no matter how
the Friendly Association might maneuver.

As Woolman's party jogged its way up the banks
of the Delaware to Easton, therefore, it was at an
instant of deceptive calm. Hostilities in the French

[2] Roy Harvey Pearce, *The Savages of America, a Study of the Indian
and the Idea of Civilization* (Baltimore: Johns Hopkins Press, 1953),
p. 35.

and Indian War had been terminated at Paris on February 10. But on April 19, Teedyuscung, the famous, unstable Delaware chieftain who was a major instrument of Pemberton policy, had been burned in his cabin during a massacre at Wyoming. The warnings of which the Pembertons had come to tell Woolman were, of course, the first inklings of Pontiac's offensive.

Nevertheless there were good reasons for Woolman to push ahead. His *Journal* account, as usual, gives the essential facts, emphasizing inward and religious ones:

Having many years felt Love in My Heart towards the Natives of this Land, who dwell far back in the Wilderness, whose Ancestors were the owners and possessors of the Country where we dwell, and who for a very small consideration assigned their Inheritance to us; and being at Philadelphia in the 8 month 1761 on a visit to some Friends who had Slaves, I fell in company with some of those Natives who lived on the East Branch of the River Susquehannah at an Indian Town called Wehalosing about 200 miles from Philadelphia. And in Conversation with them by an Interpreter, as also by observations on their Countenances and Conduct, I believed some of them were measurably acquainted with that Divine power which Subjects the rough and forward will of the Creature. And at times I felt inward drawings toward a Visit to that place of which I told none (Except my Dear Wife) until it came to Some ripeness; and then in the winter 1762 I laid it before Friends at our monthly and Quarterly and then at our General Spring meet-

ing. And having the Unity of Friends and being
thoughtful about an Indian pilot, there came a
man and 3 women from a little beyond that
Town to Philadelphia on business, and I being
acquainted thereof by letter met them in Town
in the 5 mo. 1763; and after some Conversation
finding they were Sober people I, by the Concurrence of Friends in that place, agreed to
join with them as Companions on their return. . . .

Typically, Woolman was anxious to establish
that there was nothing sudden or flighty in his
decision, that it proceeded from a sound basis in
motive and emotion, that he had good reason to
suppose from inward experience and from his repeated "Unity" with Friends that it represented
God's will, and that, given the "Concurrence" of
knowledgeable Philadelphia Friends, the journey,
while unavoidably dangerous, was not unreason-
able. What he does not say is that his prior knowledge of the Wyalusing people was fairly intimate,
certainly intriguing.

From deep in the fastnesses of "the terrible Lycoming wilderness," nearly impassable to all but
light-moving Indian messengers, traders, or war
parties on the Wyalusing Trace, there had come to
Philadelphia in 1760 an almost incredible embassy
of Christian Indians. They bore not only wampum
and good words, but three white captives to be
restored to their homes. They begged to be given
no rum and politely declined the usual presents.
Confessing to faults of Indian sharp practice in the
fur trade, they pleaded for new principles of fair
dealing on both sides. They proclaimed (at the very
height of wartime hostilities) their Christian, non-

resistant pacifism. They eagerly sought opportunities for Christian fellowship in worship and prayer; here, and again at Easton the following year, they sounded astonishingly like Quakers.

Though Quaker recorders like Woolman's dear friends Anthony Benezet and Robert Proud stressed the Friendly tone of Wyalusing talk, credit for the impetus behind the community belongs to those greatest of all Appalachian Indian missioners, the Moravians, and especially to David Zeisberger. He had converted the Wyalusing prophet Papunahung, perhaps in 1745; and Papunahung had established, as a kind of primitive Christian Seeker, his community at Wyalusing in 1752. Though it was in a Seeker's mood that Papunahung visited the Friends in 1760, the Moravians had kept in touch with him. If one senses in the situation some taint of the denominational squabbling for converts which since the Reformation has bedeviled Christian missions, the situation never became genuinely competitive. Quakers were awed and delighted by the Wyalusing spirituality. Woolman felt clear about his intent, then as ever supra-denominational:

> Love was the first motion, and then a Concern arose to Spend Some time with the Indians, that I might feel and understand their life and the Spirit they live in—if haply I might receive some Instruction from them, or they be in any degree helped forward. . . .

III

Launched on June 10, with Benjamin Parvin, a younger, stronger, and, as a surveyor, perhaps better experienced Quaker, who insisted he had a "duty" to come along into the wilderness, Woolman found crossing the frontier a reality. Too early to be a romantic lover of the natural sublime, he found crossing the Blue Ridge hard labor, "and by the roughness of the Stones, and the cavities between them, and the steepness of the hills," the works of God "in these Mountainous Deserts appeared awful." Instead of "rare" June days, he had picked a week of storm and pelting rain which drenched clothes, blankets, and tents. At his first camp grounds, the inner bark of big trees, peeled for the purpose, bore the pictographic boasts of savage forays and gave Woolman over to compassionate broodings "on the Innumerable afflictions which the proud, fierce Spirit produceth in the world."

Struggling through the next day's wet, he was overtaken by David Zeisberger, hastening again, perhaps deliberately to forestall Woolman, to Wyalusing and a hoped-for permanent mission residency there. If Zeisberger was racing Woolman, his mind was set at ease. The Woolman party dallied a day or two to let him draw ahead. But that Zeisberger had deeper urgencies became apparent when Woolman reached the Indian town of Wyoming. The Moravians had been getting the same intelligence as the Pembertons, and Wyoming news proved it sound. Rumors had come in to say that English forts were falling in the west. Warriors with bloody English scalps—tokens of war—had appeared only ten miles above Wyalusing. The population of Wyoming was getting ready to evacuate the town.

That night, Woolman got a personal sense of what it all meant. Seeing a man come and hesitate outside the door of his host's lodge, Woolman stepped out. The Indian drew a tomahawk from his blanket and balanced it in his hand. Woolman spoke quietly and stepped forward with outstretched hand —and had it clasped in greeting. Afterward he underwent the hardest test of courage—irony. Was his courage in persisting now only vanity, the fear of fear or of disgrace, "the desire of Reputation, as a man firmly settled to persevere through dangers"? Or was he still obedient to his call? A night of "painful exercize" brought him "quietness"; and he said, "therein I was renewedly confirmed that it was my duty to go forward."

So he made quiet visits with Indians cheerfully preparing to become refugees, then pushed on. Half-way to Wyalusing he met Job Chilaway, Papuna-hung's chief interpreter, whose still more disquieting news was that three warriors bound against the fort at Juniata were in the area. The thought of encountering those tigerish scalp knives tried Woolman's faith again; but his mind was renewed to quietness and he went on.

In any normal context, Wyalusing would have been extraordinary, but at this moment it was a revelation. In the midst of that wilderness "Desert" howling with fear and hatred, well-built Wyalusing was an oasis of stillness and love: "The first Indian that we Saw was a woman of modest countenance, with a Babe," who "with a harmonious voice expressed her gladness at seeing us. . . ." They were welcomed with ceremony at the regular sunset meeting of "about Sixty people, sitting in Silence"; and after a short time, Woolman wrote, "I stood up and in Some tenderness of Spirit acquainted them with the nature of my visit . . . and there appeared gladness among them." Still better, he was generously welcomed by David Zeisberger, who agreed with him the next morning that "no ill

Effects would follow" if Woolman attended the
meetings bracketing the day in which the Moravian
was preparing the people of Wyalusing for baptism or if, as Woolman wrote, "I sometimes Spake
in their meetings when love engaged me to. . . ."

No more than Woolman's own religious life or
the meetings of primitive Quakers was the life at
this instant of realization upon the threshold of
tragedy in Wyalusing cool, dry, or dumb. The
Moravian theme was religion of the heart; Quaker
"tenderness" meant sighs, tears, and a choking at the
throat. In this, Woolman, Zeisberger, and the Delawares could be at one. Unable like the Moravian
to speak the language, and with Job Chilaway
absent, Woolman finally dispensed with the labor-
ing interpreters, trusting to "the Spirit of Prayer"
when "the Current of Love" ran strong. In doing
which, he commented, "I believe the Holy Ghost
wrought on some hearts to Edification where the
words were not understood." On hearing Woolman,
Papunahung, "being then very tender," told an interpreter, "I love to feel where words come from."

Nevertheless, it did not escape Woolman that his
was not the main event in Wyalusing. Just what
tolerant David Zeisberger thought of him is hard
to tell. Zeisberger labored hard to drive Papunahung
to the classic conversion crisis. The Moravian historian, Bishop De Schweinitz, notes with approval
that Zeisberger's "fervency and joy," his power of
preaching, broke the Indians down: "Tears rolled
down their cheeks, and their whole frames were
convulsed with emotion. . . ." Papunahung's gospel
of "morality" was shattered, and Zeisberger drove
him to a "repentance . . . thorough and agonizing,"
a "distress of mind, at last . . . so great that he could
neither sleep nor eat."

Whatever else it was, this was clearly not the Quaker way. Woolman, five days before the climax of Papunahung's baptism, felt his "mind at Liberty to return." To his surprise, he found a dozen Indians anxious to go back with him on the way to Bethlehem. They knew an easier route down, and Woolman was glad for the company. At the frontier, however, he discovered why the Indians were very glad indeed to be convoyed. He and Parvin could ride ahead, and vouch for the Indians coming behind, and try to prevent trigger-happy alarm among "the outside Inhabitants."

IV

At home, John Woolman found that his first reactions to his adventure were normally personal. He strove to realize upon its religious potentialities. During the trip, he knew, "I had often been confirmed in a Belief that whatever the Lord might be pleased to allot for me would work for good. I was now careful lest I should admit any degree of Selfishness in being glad overmuch; and Laboured to Improve by these Trials in such a manner as my Gracious Father and Protector may intend for me." But he also knew that he had been presented by man and nature with new challenges to his imagination; "That people who have never been in such places, have but an Imperfect Idea of them," and their hardships. And also that he had been given new opportunities, "that I might have a quick and lively feeling of the Afflictions of my fellow-Creatures, whose Situation in life is difficult."

What had been soberly appraisable as "difficult" became, during Pontiac's War, tragic. With the officially villainous French gone, the incredibly

well organized, purely Indian power suddenly
swept over forts, taxed experienced frontier and
professional British military forces to the utmost,
kept the issue in doubt for months, and punished
with fire and fright not only the frontier but areas
which had thought themselves safe. The final result
was a kind of national decision in the long debate
over savagism, a decision later reconfirmed by the
experience of the American Revolution: the savage
was irredeemably a savage; and, in the name of God
and his civilization, the savage had to go.

Frances Parkman in *The Conspiracy of Pontiac*
cites the guilty record of panic-stricken refugees
who happened on a forest trail, to find a frontier
woman in "the Agonies of Death." She had been
"baked" and then scalped so that her brains pro-
truded onto the ground. The party debated briefly
whether to "knock her on the head"; but no one
had the courage to expose himself for that act of
mercy, and they hurried away, leaving her to rack
out the last inches of life in her exquisitely calculated "Agonies." Woolman himself the next year
(and before he had written his *Journal* account)
hired a loquacious farm helper who had been a
soldier:

> . . . And in the Evening giving a Narrative of
> his Captivity amongst the Indians, he informed
> me that he saw two of his fellow Captives
> Tortured to Death, One of which being tied
> to a Tree had abundance of pine Splinters run
> into his Body and then set on fire, and that
> this was Continued at times near two Days
> before he died. That they opened the Belly of
> the other and fastened a part of his Bowels to
> a Tree, and then Whipped the Poor Creature

till by his running around the Tree his bowels
were drawn out of his Body.

The world of gentle John Woolman was by no
means innocent of the knowledge of pain and
terror.

Hundreds of such stories of surprise, slaughter,
rapine, torment, murder, captivity, abuse, and hu-
miliation lost nothing in the telling. With all sorts
of minglings of fiction and of sadism and guilt, they
amounted finally to a legend of sheer horror. They
established decisively the frontier axiom: "The only
good Indian is a dead Indian." In frontier minds,
many of them affected by Scotch-Irish Calvinism,
arose a myth, as a pseudotheological rationalization
of that hatred, which varied the familiar myth that
Americans were led in the wilderness like the children of Israel to the Promised Land. This myth said
that Indians were cursed Canaanites, and it had
become the sacred duty of God's people to stamp
them out.

What the Quakers and Moravians were up
against, in other words, once Pontiac had launched
his bolt, was a growing intention of genocide.
John Woolman's moment of visit to Wyalusing was
timed, perhaps intuitively, during the last historical
moment in North America at which the dreams of
John Eliot, David Zeisberger, and the Quakers
could really be thought to be viable. The prudence
of the Wyalusings in using Woolman and Parvin
for convoy across the frontier had been well advised. In August came the first massacre of Moravian Indians by Scotch-Irish militia. By December
the Moravian Indians were disarmed and concen-
trated in a camp on Province Island in the river east
of Philadelphia, Papunahung and Chilaway, to the

astonishment of authorities, having brought in the Wyalusings. The Conestoga Indians, defenseless pacifists, had been massacred by white men at Lancaster; and Philadelphia was threatened with siege by hysterical "Paxton Boy" insurrectionists demanding the scalps of the praying Indians and the necks of Israel Pemberton and a selection of other Quakers.

The "Paxton Boys" were perhaps the biggest lynch mob in the history of the country. That they were denied and dispersed by governmental firmness and Franklin's diplomacy, so that no Quaker was hanged and half the Indians survived their psychic and other prison diseases, was important but not entirely consoling. When John Woolman came finally to account for his whole experience— of which this aftermath that he never mentioned formed a part—what was he to make of it all? What could the Quaker Saint conclude?

v

The *Journal* account makes it clear that Woolman did not hesitate to confront ideas or probe for meaning. Some readers have been disappointed by his insistence on abstracting instead of describing precisely the details which he left largely inferential. Yet, in the long run the significance of this pilgrim's progress, and of this pilgrim, depends not on the fact that he went to the Indians, but on the meaning he can help us to see.

Woolman wrote and rewrote his *Journal* in the next several years, and late in 1763 he finished one of the strongest and best of his essays, *A Plea for the Poor*, and included the Indian. In neither did he indulge in the gestures of the modern, ritualistic liberal. He was no bleeding heart, banqueting on a guilty contention that Indians were nice and sweet and wholly in the right, or, if not so, wholly to be condoned, "understood," and explained, where whites were unforgivable villains. He had seen in prospect the painted war party rise in his path, muscular and deft, eager for blood, delighted with pain, implacably set on the destruction of the defenseless Woolman and Parvin. He had been really scared for good reasons.

Neither was Woolman an elephant washer, lost in the Sisyphean tasks of point-by-point solutions of innumerable, hopelessly knotted contingencies. He started and ended in real considerations, and he saw that real, specific reforms were needed. But he understood the situation and its problems in general terms, in abstractions, ideas, general principles to which he could be committed in reason, faith, and emotion. He abdicated neither the head, the heart, nor the soul; neither God nor man. The key to it all, he became convinced, was at once moral and psychological, a question of the spirit— the habit of mind—in which things were done. From that spirit both justice and love were absent because men put themselves before God.

From first to last, it must be observed, Woolman's errand to Wyalusing was a venture in religious obedience. He went in the assurance that God meant him to go, and his courage there and back was renewed in the assurance not that he would be physically safe but that his journey was apostolic. Speaking in a meeting of Young Quakers just before he left for Wyalusing, he was "led" to point out that some of the disciples Christ had prayed to have kept from evil were "met with great hardships and Afflictions in this world, and at last

Suffered death by Cruel men"; therefore, "it appears that whatsoever befalls men while they live in pure Obedience to God, as it certainly works for good, so it may not be considered an evil as it relates to them." And that was his own "spirit" throughout.

In those wild "back parts," however, there clearly was present, terrible evil. How to explain it? Woolman's answer was emergent and finally profound. Selling rum to Indians was "a great evil":

First they being thereby deprived of the use of their Reason and their spirits violently agitated, quarrels often arise . . . and . . . bitterness and resentments: again, their Skins and furs, gotten through much fatigue and hard travels in hunting . . . when they begin to be Intoxicated they often sell at a low rate for more rum; and afterward when they suffer for want of the necessaries of life, are angry. . . .

But it was usual everywhere to put the blame on the poor, "hardened and Corrupt" Indian trader. It was like John Woolman to see further than that:

I also remembered that the people on the frontier among whom this evil is too common are often poor people who venture to the outside of a Colony that they may live more independent on Such who are wealthy, who often set high rents on their Land, being renewedly confirmed in a belief, that if all our inhabitants lived according to pure wisdom, Labouring to promote Universal Love and Righteousness, and ceased from every inordinate desire after wealth, and from all customs

which are Tinctured with Luxury, the way
would be Easier . . . to live comfortably on
Honest Employments, without . . . being drawn
into schemes to make settlements on Lands
which have not been honestly purchased of the
Indians, or of applying to that wicked practice
of Selling rum to them.

In short, no man could escape from his complicity
except by facing up to it. Woolman's basic insight
was that the same "proud, fierce Spirit" which sent
Indians on the warpath, and "their restless, unquiet
state of mind who live in this Spirit, and . . . the
hatred which mutually grows up in the minds of the
children of those Nations Engaged in war with each
other" as equally afflicted frontiersmen as Indians,
civilized settlers as frontiersmen, imperial Europe-
ans as colonists, landlords as tenants, merchants as
slaveholders—every kind of oppressor or would-be
oppressor. He felt a growing compassion for the
Indians. Not denying the theses that the natural
bounty was more truly used by white agrarian than
by Indian hunting culture or that God's providence
had led the Quakers to Pennsylvania, Woolman
found a middle ground in holding that full, honest
use must be made by the whites of the land they
had been given before they put any more pressure
on the Indian.

He feared that the Indians had been painfully
cheated of a fair inheritance on the coast. And as
he rode through their present "Mountains, Swamps,
and Barren deserts," the eye of his imagination was
opened to a vision of tragic responsibility:

I had a prospect of the English along the
Coast for upwards of nine hundred miles

[21]

where I have traveled. And the favourable Situation of the English, and the difficulties attending the natives and the Slaves amongst us, were open to me, and a weighty and Heavenly care came over my mind, and love filled my heart toward all mankind, in which I felt a Strong Engagement that we might . . . so attend to pure Universal Righteousness as to give no just cause of offence to the gentiles who do not profess christianity, whether the Blacks from Africa, or the Native Inhabitants of this Continent. And here I was led into a close, laborious Enquiry, whether I as an individual kept clear from all things which tended to stir up, or were connected with wars, Either in this Land or Africa. And my heart was deeply concerned that in the future I might in all things keep steadily to the pure Truth, and live and walk in the plainness and Simplicity of a Sincere follower of Christ. And in this lonely Journey, I did this day greatly bewail the spreading of a wrong Spirit, believing that the prosperous Convenient Situation of the English, requires a Constant Attention to Divine love and wisdom, to guide and Support us in a way answerable to the will of that Good, Gracious and Almighty Being who hath an Equal regard to all mankind. And here Luxury and Covetousness, with the numerous Oppressions and other evils attending them, appeared very Afflicting to me, and I felt in that which is Immutable that the Seeds of a great Calamity and desolation are Sown and growing fast on this Continent. Nor have I words sufficient to set forth that longing I then felt, that we who are placed along the Coast, and have tasted the

Love and Goodness of God, might arise in his
Strength, and like faithful Messengers Labour
to check the growth of those Seeds that they
may not ripen to the Ruin of our posterity.

The only response which seemed adequate was the
performance, for values however merely symbolic,
of his painful and dangerous "Concern to Spend
Some time with the Indians, that I might feel and
understand their life, and the Spirit they live in";
his "desire to cherish the Spirit of Love and peace
amongst these people. . . ."

VI

At the end one asks: Was Woolman's gesture to
the Indians, in the face of historical tragedy, adequate? It could not in any case have been fateful.
He was not visiting the Senecas but Wyalusing; not
Pontiac but Papunahung. And he could not save
even the Christian Indians. That part of the conti-
nental and eventually national tragedy which he
foresaw fell inexorably. But then, is it really given to
any individual alone, or to mankind itself, to forestall tragedy, conquer evil? Woolman's solution was
to find where the faults lay, to undertake to correct
them in his own heart and complicitly in the hearts
of his fellows, and to trust in God to bring his en-
deavor to a good end.

We have heard a great deal in recent years about
"the end of American innocence." In the light of
thought like Woolman's it may be considered one
of Reinhold Niebuhr's ironies of American history
that, since the birth of the Republic, there should
ever have flourished such an "innocence" as we have

been shocked two centuries after to have seen fore-
closed.

In his own time, it may be asked whether Woolman did not escape Professor Pearce's dilemma by
a method not dreamed of in modern culturological
philosophy. To be sure, Woolman produced no new,
major intellectual synthesis to solve the problems
of cross-cultural complexity. But in the infinitely
more sophisticated two centuries since, as events
make clearer every day all over the world, nobody
else has performed that feat. Current history suggests that the century which discovered sweet culturological reasonableness will be known as an age
of almost universal tragedy. It would appear that to
possess the power to wage war, whether ideological,
national, tribal, or even genocidal, is to be almost
irresistibly tempted to do it.

Woolman's solutions have the ring of validity for
his own time. We look back and assent: Yes, it
could have worked; and history would have been
different. But then we ask again: Could it have
worked only for a society of saints? To a Christian,
John Woolman might suggest perspectives so faithful and "primitive" as to seem fresh and disturbing,
if not shocking. Can one still sound the depths of
his heart, be possessed in his imagination, find that
unsettling peace which is the will of God and will
order our lives and affect the course of history in
our time, as Woolman undertakes to show?

On the other hand, to return at last to Eric Hoffer
and his persistent, perhaps tongue-in-cheek, link-
ages of Judeo-Christian with Nazi, Jacobin, and
Bolshevik examples of fanaticism, we are also forced
to look at Woolman and his saintliness from non-
Christian perspectives. To take Hoffer's line of
sight, it is clear that Woolman's ideas and actions

conform to the patterns of Hoffer's true believers nowhere in origin, expression, or effect. Woolman's way with life is an entirely different way of addressing oneself to those problems of human frustration which produce Hoffer's fanatics. Without necessary reference to Christianity (though finally depending on some sort of religious insight), through Woolman we are pointed toward other and essentially American traditions.

Disregarding sainthood, Woolman's way marches toward the center of major American traditions which assert that a happy, successful people need not be cynical, static, or stagnant; that agents of change need not be desperate frustrates, charging into destruction because any change is better than failure, guilt, and rot. These are traditions of minds as good; spirits as elevated; and careers as effective as those of Franklin, Washington, Jefferson, Emerson, Lincoln, Whitman, the Roosevelts, and Kennedy. They insist, with Poor Richard, that it is hard for an empty bag to stand upright and that without uprightness no good result can follow. They say, "Produce great persons, all the rest follows." They carry forward Emerson's message to the young men of America: You must create the good society, the truths of an age, the beauty of an era by yourselves and for yourselves in your own time.

Centrally this all became, in the end, a tradition of individualism based not upon "inner-directedness," but upon faith and upon individual reliance in spiritual powers flowing within the nature of things and the true inward life of man. These powers were Jefferson's "Nature" and Emerson's "Oversoul," as they appear to be Paul Tillich's "God." At once immanent and transcendent, they are also the "Pure Principle" of Woolman's life. Ultimately this

[25]

tradition envisages a society dominated by free-standing but God-directed individuals; a society continuously renovated, reformed, even re-created in the mass or (to use Whitman's words) in the "En-masse" by the cumulative creativity of "simple, separate persons." In short, there is in the long run nothing so queer, sectarian, or historically remote about Woolman's saintliness. Perhaps it was, as he hoped, extraordinarily "pure." Nonetheless it represents and participates in a central American tradition and doctrine.

For us the essential question regarding Woolman's way and its tradition seems to be one of availability. We are offered a nonfanatical, non-"mass movement" way of solving social and cultural problems like those of disinherited poverty, public education, and civil rights. Basically, as we shall see, Woolman's way is also that of men like the Rev. Dr. Martin Luther King. If King is Woolman's sort of true believer, we have had ample reason to be aware of the threats to King and his way from Hoffer's kind of true believer. Woolman's way depends upon the appeal, not from frustration to fanatic spoliation, nor from God the "Wholly Other" to a humanly impossible sainthood; but upon an appeal from common citizen conscience to conscience shared in a scrupulous and responsible individuality. Perhaps what John Woolman has most to say to us is to be sensitive and to care.

Chapter II

SPIRITUAL ANCESTRY

Before I was seven years old, I began to be
acquainted with the operations of Divine Love.
. . . My Parents having a large family of children, used frequently on first-days after meeting to put us to read in the Holy Scriptures, or
some religious books . . . From what I had read,
I believed there had been in past ages, people
who Walked in Uprightness before God in a
degree exceeding any that I knew, or heard of,
now living: and the Apprehension of there being less Steadiness and firmness amongst people in this age than in past ages, often Troubled me while I was still young.

With every allowance for individual difference,
the common sense that knowledge of background
makes the right base for understanding people is
doubtless correct. When we ask how he became
John Woolman, it is to begin to answer the real
question: What kind of mind was this, really? Intellectually, it's a wise child indeed that knows its
ancestral tree. Woolman's thought, however, traces
to one unmistakable potency. His spiritual ancestor
was the founder of Quakerism, a peer, after his
fashion, of Cromwell, Milton, and Bunyan—marvelous George Fox. After Fox it was the apostles of

early, militant Quakerism, especially William Penn. And after them, those who were Woolman's physical as well as spiritual progenitors, his frontier Quaker parents.

Shakespeare, obsessed with order, might easily have imagined the turmoil of the two generations after his death, during which the structure of the English realm was shattered by religious civil war and the King himself judicially executed. What he could never have guessed was the creativity which the same convulsions called forth. The character of the nation changed. Shakespeare's divinity which hedged a king was smashed and replaced by political innovations which, three centuries later, retain potentialities not fully explored. In a spectrum ranging from Milton to Bunyan, unpredictable expressive powers were released. Most fatefully, the brooding, boiling religious tensions of England exploded. They burst into chaos, as had often been forecast. But they also unexpectedly released energies which shaped the forms of English religious life into institutions strangely fluid and more dynamic than any before them.

I

Among all the phenomena of seventeenth-century English religion, none was at once so exotic and effective as George Fox. The son of a weaver called "Righteous Christer," Fox was born in Drayton-in-the-Clay (Fenney Drayton), Leicestershire, in 1624. Perhaps because Fox's mother was, as William Penn said, "a woman accomplished above most of her degree in the place where she lived," young George got a good lower-middle-class education. But he was of the people, and part of his power stemmed from that. As the genteel Penn acknowledged, "The side of his understanding which lay next to the world, and especially the expression of it, might sound uncouth and unfashionable." Fox was a master of folk debate and marketplace repartee. "No arts or parts had any share in the matter or manner of his ministry," continued Penn:

So that as to men he was an original being no man's copy. . . . He was of an innocent life, no busy body, nor self-seeker, neither touchy nor critical: what fell from him was very inoffensive, if not very edifying. So meek, contented, modest, easy, steady, tender it was a pleasure to be in his company . . . and I can say I never saw him out of his place, or not a match for every service or occasion.

For in all things he acquitted himself like a man, yea a strong man, a new and heavenly-minded man. A divine, and a naturalist, and all of God Almighty's making. I have been surprised at his questions and answers in natural things, that whilst he was ignorant of useless and sophistical science, he had in him the foundation of useful and commendable knowledge, and cherished it everywhere. Civil beyond all forms of breeding in his behavior; very temperate, eating little and sleeping less, though a bulky person.

Some sense of Fox's innate intellectual brilliance comes out in Penn's words, but almost nothing of the Dionysian, almost berserk incandescence with which Fox met the challenges of his time. In one of the great ages of mysticism he became one of its foremost contemplatives.[1] Yet among mystics he was also one of the great activists. He preached, journeyed, suffered, endured, and triumphed with a force which seems superhuman. Repeatedly, hostile but sensitive disputants begged him to take his eyes off them, they pierced them so. Fox must have been an impressive physical specimen. He traveled the roads of England tirelessly, sleeping out in all weathers in his leather suit. He was repeatedly mobbed, beaten up, bloodied, knocked unconscious, and so bruised he could not turn himself in bed. His recoveries were apparently rapid and the effects upon his will and spirit nothing.

There was something deeply gracious, spiritually courageous, and mystical about all this in Fox. But there was something more than militant, too. He was aggressive, deliberately provocative, implacable. He would not strike back, he was cheerful, but he must have been maddening. He simply looked down drawn swords and pistols. He merely declined a commission in Cromwell's army. He went where he was warned not to go. He walked into buzzing "steeple-houses," bearded formidable Puritan "priests" in their pulpits, caused riots, was beaten up, and walked right back as soon as he was able. He took imprisonment calmly, disputed his judges with embarrassing acuteness, and survived months and years of prison conditions designed rather to destroy than to punish him. His was indeed the state of the evangelical soul at war.

---

[1] Evelyn Underhill, *Mysticism* (New York: Noonday Press, 1955), pp. 454, 469–70.

II

What Fox was at war about, however, distinguishes him sharply from any number of prophets and agitators. Behind him lay an intense and genuine religious experience which his first-rate mind had translated into a set of important ideas. And, as Penn also testifies, Fox had no intention or desire to exploit his mysticism, his ideas, his strength, or his extraordinary charisma for personal advantage. He believed that the truth would make men free, and he seems as purely as is humanly possible to have wished to free them. He was a seeker, votary, and adept; then missionary and prophet; finally, if informally, bishop of his Religious Society of Friends. He never sought to be Lord Bishop. His comment dictated for his *Journal* after a visit to New England in 1672 was typical. His preaching had so impressed "some of the magistrates" in Rhode Island that they said, " 'If they had money enough, they would hire me to be their minister.' " Fox's response was to feel that then it was time for him to go: " '. . . for if their eye was so much to me, or any of us, they would not come to their own teacher.' For this thing (hiring ministers) had spoiled many, by hindering them from improving their own talents, whereas our labour is to bring every one to their own teacher in themselves."

This notion of everyone's own teacher within himself was Fox's basic idea. It has long passed current in Quaker thought under the title of "the Inner Light," though Fox himself settled on no one term for it. He referred to it variously as the "Seed," "Word," or "Voice," or "that of God in every man." He had in mind what has traditionally been called

the Quaker verse of the New Testament (John 1:9):
"That was the true Light, which lighteth every man
that cometh into the world." Or as Fox essentially
paraphrased the verse in recording his most striking
mystical experience, "The Lord God opened to me
by his invisible power, how 'every man was enlightened by the divine light of Christ.' I saw it
shine through all . . ."

Thought like that of Fox, of course, had many
roots. As Rufus Jones has shown, some of these went
deep into the furthest reaches of Western religion
in its mystical phases. Others sprang more directly
from the old, submerged heritages of antinomian
religion in England—the Lollards, the Brownists.
Still others were immediately present in the caldron
of Cromwellian England with its "Enthusiasm,"
Seekers, Familists, Ranters, Muggletonians. Fox and
Quakerism would have been unimaginable without
Puritanism and the Puritan revolution. And in one
sense they were a virtual terminus of Puritanism,
of the dissidence of dissent, the ultimate in purify-
ing reductivity.

On the other hand, the revolt of Quakerism
against Puritanism and all that Puritanism distinctively stands for theologically was so total that the
Quakers were early seen to have come back almost
full circle to Catholicism. It was not infrequently
charged in Commonwealth and Restoration days
that the Quakers were Papists in disguise. And the
canard was long a-dying that William Penn himself
was a Jesuit spy and intriguer. Insofar as Catholics,
Anglicans, Puritans, and Quakers were all Christians, the likenesses among them were naturally
overwhelmingly more important than the differences. Nevertheless, in a political age hypersensitive
to religious distinctions, the differences between

Quakerism and Puritanism were significant enough to be distressing to both sides. Almost everyone now agrees that Puritan and Anglican resort to persecution of the Quakers was as wrong as the Quakers supposed. Still, it is true that if any of the three had finally succeeded in its aim, it would have destroyed the others. Since in one sense Quakerism belonged with Puritanism, it is instructive to look at their differences.

One way of making sense of Puritanism is to see that as a way of religion (as distinct from a mere way of theology) it was founded upon a structure of myths. By "myth" here is meant neither lies nor archetypes, but that fusion of idea and emotion in some sharp, dramatic image upon which men's convictions become grounded and through which their hopes, visions, and commitments are expressed. Puritanism was grounded on perhaps half a dozen of these. The first was that of the Hebraic, monolithic Jehovah, lost in ineffable majesty and blinding purity, knowable only through the condescension of His grace to man His creature. Second, the myth of Adam's Fall, to the Puritan a fall to total depravity, with all natural grace of reason or spiritual apprehension burned to dust and cinders. Third, the historical vision of God's covenants with man in Adam, Noah, Abraham, Jacob, Moses, the kings and prophets, and finally Christ—each broken, betrayed, and despised by fallen man, whose every best thought was naturally a rebellion and a sin.

The fourth and the most determinative of the Puritan's myths was that of the Primitive Church. According to his standard of the Primitive Church, derived from the New Testament, he wished to purify, ceasing at his own point of revolutionary arrest, the Catholic, Anglican, Presbyterian, or whatever

[33]

church. To make the Primitive Church the church of the living present the Puritan yearned, suffered, and if need be died. In seeking to live for and within that Church he exercised two final, interpenetrating myths: the myth of the Calling, and the myth of the present Covenant. Calling presupposed an immanent, personally directed providence of God which elected the saved to grace and directed them as strangers and sojourners through their pilgrims' progress in a world estranged from God. Interwoven and sometimes indistinguishable was the myth of the present Covenant: tribally men might strike bargains with God to serve Him and be His people; socially and governmentally groups or institutions might do the same; so might individual persons.

The Quaker in Commonwealth and Restoration England found himself persecuted by Puritan and Anglican alike. But nowhere was his persecution more indignantly implacable, or more revealing, than in Puritan New England. There his difference was plainly intolerable because it struck at the heart of the New England Way. The founding fathers of the Massachusetts Bay theocracy had, in the beginning, found it necessary to purge themselves of antinomian Anne Hutchinson and her followers, even at the cost of disciplining their greatest minister, John Cotton. Their narrower, pettier sons had no weapons but exile, flogging, and the halter for the terrifying Quaker missionaries, all zeal and fervor, who burst upon them a generation later.

What was the trouble? The Quaker shared cordially in the myths of Calling, Covenant, Covenants, and Primitive Church. To be sure, his Primitive Church was almost wholly noninstitutional. But that fact distressed in the Puritan only what moved him to anguish and fury in the Quaker rejection of the Puritan interpretation of the myths of the monolithic Jehovah and the Fall of man. Long troubled by doctrines of depravity and damnation, George Fox had responded prophetically with a vision of the world wherein, as he said, "I saw . . . that there was an ocean of darkness and death; but an infinite ocean of light and love, which flowed over the ocean of darkness." He insisted upon the existence, potential and actual, of something of God, the Light of heaven, the indwelling Christ, in every man. He insisted that earnest seeking and discipline made the immediate experience, more real than any mere outward or "creaturely" experience of God Within, available to every human being. He insisted that man was still made, as from the beginning, in the image of God and that the meaning of this was that God was to be found within his heart. For Fox this never implied any lessening of the generally Puritan sensitivity, even agony, of conscience or lessening of moral strenuousness. Quite the contrary. But it scrapped much of the distinctively Puritan feeling for the nature and condition of man and man's world.

Supported swiftly by able followers, the missionizing, expanding, interpreting, prophetic "Publishers of Truth," Fox developed his spiritual insights into revolutionary codes of behavior. Some of these now seem trivial, some still significant; but almost all were shocking in the beginning. In a surprisingly short time they had been rationalized into a system about as consistent as cultural expressions of ideas ever become.

The great central concern was to so cultivate the experience of the inner light as to set it in entire governance of the lives of the Religious Society of

Friends and its individual members. To begin with, every institutional hindrance to that perfect dominion had to be done away with. Therefore, Fox and his followers became enemies to institutional religion—to "steeple-houses," to "hireling ministers," and to "professors," or those who taught an abstract, dogmatic, nonexperiential Christianity. They also fell at enmity with the political institutionalization of religion, with every manifestation of religious establishment. They refused to pay tithes. Most inconveniently, they refused to take oaths in court or in connection with any legal proceeding. This action often deprived them of protection and made them liable to the wrath of the law. But the Scripture said, "Swear not at all," and it said that one's aye should be aye and one's nay, nay, and taking oaths identified state with church. So the Friends became nonjurors.

For the plastic glories of art and architecture they substituted the plain, square meetinghouse. For the liturgical glories of music, chant, procession, form, rite, literature, and vestment they substituted silence. The silent meeting aimed not to cultivate even meditation but to subdue it. Not only the body but the carnal mind was to be disciplined, suppressed, and got out of the way so that the light within might grow and dominate. Therefore the mutual cultivation of such a silence within a meeting might become the most important thing that happened there. If one were moved to pray or prophesy aloud, one must "clear himself" and do so. To refuse was to violate and deny the light. But to go so much as a syllable beyond what one had plainly been given to say was equally a violation. One could only be as sensitive to inward reality and as responsible to its leadings as one could make oneself. In this as in everything, the Quaker's sensitivity to conscience and to mystic experience became central.

This sensitivity and this force of inner event, though of the essence, had to be balanced against responsibility to the group, the community. Communally, Quaker insights became institutionalized as "testimonies." Individually, one's experience, conscientiously pursued, might eventuate in "concerns." Some of the most difficult and troublesome of the testimonies went under the heading of simplicity and plainness. The world of the seventeenth century was minutely hierarchical. And it was heir to innumerable extravagant ceremonies by which hierarchical gradations were recognized and the vanity which supported them mollified. To the furious incredulity of their relations and neighbors, the Friends rejected the whole body of prideful social form. They refused "hat honor," declining to remove their hats in church, before kings, nobles, and other social superiors, before magistrates, and even before parents. They insisted upon returning to the traditional form of the second personal singular pronoun, declining to address in courtesy any person as if he were plural and therefore confining singular personal address to "thee," and "thou," instead of "you." And they held to other forms of plain speech in an era enthusiastically devoted not only to titles but to elegant circumlocution. Every title of worldly distinction was sunk in the appellation "Friend," and they joined other radical sectaries in abolishing the pagan names of the days and the months and substituting numbers for them.

As one reads the history of the early persecutions of the Quakers for insisting upon the letter of such prohibitions, one is sometimes moved to wonder at the need for such rigidities. Nevertheless those "testimonies" really did point to fundamental insights. What on the surface might seem petty, even arrogant, when persevered in as type and symbol of basic truth, revealed ideas of a significance so revolutionary as never yet to have been fully grasped in modern culture. What the Quakers testified to was the unique value and absolute equality of the human spirit, of that of God in every person. And they found means to express those insights more important than anything one did or did not do with his hat.

One distinctive and enduring Quaker testimony has been pacifism. Quakers supposed that the inner light impelled them to peace, to suffering rather than wielding violence, to living constructively, to aligning themselves with life, not death. And they grew progressively into a sense that the seed of God within every other man must be held sacred. Therefore they abjured violence and refused military service, beginning with Fox's decision to be returned to jail rather than accept a Cromwellian commission. Therefore they were pioneering feminists, thinking it absurd that there should be any less of the light in woman than in man. From the beginning their women testified, prophesied, ministered, and took the lead wherever they were inwardly empowered to do so. They were spared the follies which from the Schoolmen to the Victorians sought to justify the denial of entire humanity to women. On the same bases, the Friends became early and natural humanitarians. It was not merely that their own sufferings taught them to be compassionate. They saw with widening sensitivity that hunger, privation, injustice, and ignorance oppressed the seed of

God in sufferers. Obviously it was their business to lift such oppression.

Inevitably the Quakers also became involved in the much-discussed "Protestant ethic." Even further than the Puritans they were enjoined against conspicuous consumption, and their communal testimony to plainness eventuated in the famous Quaker garb which fossilized into a uniform. If the Quaker shopkeeper at first lost trade in consequence of dispensing with civilities, he soon more than made it up by his reputation for honesty, for a fixed price at a fair profit margin, and for the reliability of his goods. Thrift, sobriety, hard work, and good reputation helped him make more than enough to pay the persecuting penalties levied upon him. But then the question became: what to do with the profits? His was, in fairly extreme form, the general Protestant problem of the "weaned affections." By learning to care and not to care, to follow his calling hard in this world so as to prosper truly in the next, the Quaker businessman was severely exposed to the classic temptations. He had to "keep low" carefully not to be overcome. Early in the history of the Society there began to come warnings against too much devotion to worldly things, against giving way to acquisitive temptations. In the long run, worldly success would prove far more dangerous to Quakerism than the worst of its worldly persecution.

III

Before the birth of John Woolman in 1720, the Religious Society of Friends had passed through two distinct periods in its history and was well into a third. There had been the intensely prophetic opening of the movement as the "Publishers of Truth"

carried their gospel to the "Children of the Light."
This had been characterized by an emotional fervor
not seldom bordering on the fanatic, and by a spiritual depth which gathered a painfully persecuted
people into an effective religious body. Necessarily
this was followed by a time of organization and consolidation as that body was converted into its peculiar version of a church. And with institutionalization
came the inevitable concomitants of group organization or, in short, politics. There were quarrels,
debates, divisions, and, inescapably, schisms. Inevitably also, such events led to a tightening of discipline. Suddenly, instead of the glorious simplicity
of the burning word of God, free in the world and
mediated through their lives, the Quakers had upon
their hands all the exasperating responsibilities ordinary to institutions.

Their problems were further complicated because
their society and its constituency were in open,
avowed, necessary opposition to much in the normal
patterns of the culture around them. They found it
impossible in the long run not to adopt the normal
defenses of the radical minority group which was
determined to preserve its character intact. They
began to form a cultural enclave. Even before the
death of Margaret Fell Fox, that Mother of the
movement was protesting the growing legalism, the
negativism and rigidity, the Levitical quality which
increasingly structured Quaker discipline was taking
on. Outwardly and societally among the Friends,
a new sort of Pharisaism sprang up to protect the
workings of the light within. But it was becoming a
serious question whether that protection did not
rather threaten to eclipse than to foster the light.
Nowhere was this more true than in the Quaker
relationship to the life of the mind. For obvious

reasons Quakers early became concerned with an education of their children which was, for practical purposes, parochial. In dealing particularly with young children their doctrines of leading out the light within gave them fine advantages. They could and did make significant advances toward a "natural" education—"natural" both in permitting the child to realize upon his inward nature through education and in bringing the child close to nature and natural process, so that a surprisingly large number of Friends became early scientists.

On the other hand, the drawing of the walls of the enclave closer about the Society and its people was to have disastrous consequences for its intellectual life. A doctrine of truth inwardly known by mystical practices easily produces anti-intellectualism. The prophetic Friends were not unlike the poets of romanticism in preaching the heart over the head. Later Quakers began to declaim, even legislate against what was "heady." When their disciplines began to hedge about the heart as well, the evangelical power and even the "birthright" appeal of their religious movement were bound to decline sadly.

IV

As historians like Brinton, Tolles, and James have helped us to see, however, the Quakers within the Pennsylvania–West New Jersey radius of Penn's "Holy Experiment" passed through an era actually far more complex than an older, linear explanation of Quaker history allowed for. The time was as heavily laden with ironies as any in the American history of paradoxes. And it coincided largely with the lifetime of John Woolman.

The standard tradition has seen only Quaker decadence during the eighteenth century. A period of consolidation and withdrawal follows the blazing evangelism of the age of Fox. Religious retreat into quietism, ecclesiastical retreat into rigid discipline focused upon petty detail, and defeat by the business ethic are supposed to have turned the Quakers into "bourgeoisie"—into, as an old joke puts it with epigrammatic drive, "a God-fearing, money-making people." William Comfort tells the story of a tourist through the ecclesiastical zoo of tolerant Pennsylvania who came at last upon Philadelphia and its Quakers in their strange uniform:

"And who are these?"
"These are the Quakers."
"Indeed, and what do they believe?"
"They believe in six per cent irredeemable ground-rents." [2]

Quite clearly there is solid truth in these traditions. The utopianism of the "Holy Experiment" in Philadelphia, like that of Byllynge's "Concessions" in West New Jersey, failed swiftly. It failed partly because of William Penn's absenteeism and inconsistencies, but mostly because it wasn't "holy." Almost at once Utopia's people, typically American, became given to the personal pursuit of prosperity, to Quaker-Whig political attitudes, to frontier independence, and to an unholy degree of hell-raising. Utopia in dying left important legacies of ideas like toleration, peace, and humanity. It made Pennsylvania a haven for the oppressed and the non-English. And it left, as we have seen, possibilities for

[2] William Wistar Comfort, *Just Among Friends: The Quaker Way of Life* (New York: The Macmillan Company, 1941), p. 87.

a Quaker culture which were all too humanly comprised at the roots.

The pattern is the same as for New England. There the death of the theocracy left behind its legacy of Yankee culture. Utopia, as it has always turned out to be, was nowhere. But the culture of a post-utopian people became definitely something in a real geographic setting. Without, perhaps, being sufficiently aware of the paradoxes in which he is dealing, Howard Brinton argues persuasively that in the actual sequence of the periods of Quaker history, after the "heroic or apostolic period," during which there was a "synthesis or balance of mysticism and evangelicalism, about 1650–1790," there followed "the period of cultural creativeness," which was also a "period of greater mystical inwardness, about 1700–1800." The "period of conflict and decline" he would not place until the nineteenth century. Quakerism during the eighteenth century, he points out, "developed a distinctive cultural pattern . . . a Quaker was distinguishable by the way he talked, dressed and behaved." This was "the Golden Age of Quakerism in America," and the flowering of Quaker culture took place most intensively in "life itself in home, meeting, and community." [3]

Lacking wars, disasters, and atrocities, and being noncombative and nonromantic, the Quaker frontier experience has been largely overlooked, as indeed the historical life of the middle colonies has generally been overshadowed by that of New England and Virginia. Yet the Quaker frontier was perhaps more immediately, more significantly successful in its mission than any other. If the frontier was

---

[3] Howard Brinton, *Friends for 300 Years* (New York: Harper & Row Publishers, Inc., 1952), pp. 96–7, 175–6, 181–6.

the line demarcating the wilderness from civilization, its true mission was not to fight Indians or to
lay nature waste. Its mission was to civilize. And
this aim the West New Jersey and east-of-the-moun-
tains Pennsylvania Quaker frontier achieved superbly. Its tasks took muscle, adaptability, ingenuity,
and perseverance. They also required intelligence,
integrity, good will, discipline—and a devotion to
the life of the spirit on the part of its almost totally
common-man constituency as impressive in its way
as that of New England. Of all this John Woolman
was the son and heir.

V

Where George Fox represents the Dionysian re-
belliousness and spiritual warfare of his century,
Woolman represents the Apollonian peaceableness,
measure, and restraint of the eighteenth century.
But he represents these things with a Quaker difference which makes him radically distinct from
such contemporaries as Benjamin Franklin and
Jonathan Edwards. Woolman was able to become
genuinely creative as a Quaker because he was
solidly based in the best of a culture rich in achieved
tradition, custom, and expression. Quaker frontier
success had been, in the very generation of his
father, simultaneous with a unique success in creating Quaker culture. It was Woolman's good fortune
to be reared at the heart of both sorts of success:
on the country periphery, where the luxury of distance from the corruptions of power struggles and
city worldliness afforded him in youth the happy
innocence of cultural purity.

The first American Woolman, John Woolman's
grandfather, also John, came to West New Jersey in

1678 as a substantial citizen, a Proprietor of the colony, and eventually a large landholder. Though trained to the weaver's trade, he cleared land vigorously for a "plantation" and built a fine brick house on the banks of the Rancocas River in Burlington County. There Elizabeth Borton Woolman bore him five daughters and a son, Samuel, to whom the house and lands were left.

Samuel, like his father a man of substance in the economic, political, and religious life of the community, sired a large family. His wife, Elizabeth (Burr), bore seven sons and six daughters and lived with frontier vigor to her seventy-eighth year. The atmospheres of Samuel's home were much more than farmerish or simple. They were literate, the children being taught to read at the earliest possible age and encouraged, even exercised, in the use of the family library of religion, surveying, and law. They were responsible: the boys were taught mensuration, the drawing of wills and handling of estates, merchandising and accounting, and practical medicine as well as good citizenship. And they were substantial, not merely pious, in religion.

Though the Rancocas meeting was rural enough, through Burlington the Woolmans came into intimate contact with the great world of their culture. Burlington was a bustling center of the international Quakerism of the Atlantic Culture. From 1684 until 1760 the Yearly Meeting, the ultimate Quaker synod of the whole region, alternated between Philadelphia and Burlington, twenty miles apart. It was a period of great traveling by "the leading Friends"; so much so that, as Brinton remarks, "Several could say toward the end of their lives that they had visited every meeting in the Society of Friends." [4]

---

[4] *Ibid.* p. 186.

The great preachers came through Burlington as a matter of course and found the fellowship thriving. There, too, the Woolmans built family friendships, with, for instance, the cultivated, bookish, politically powerful Smiths. With their money and land, their intelligence and cultivation, their influence, responsibility, and service, in short, the Woolmans of Rancocas would have been fairly typical American country gentry of the eighteenth century had they not been Quakers.

That they were not only Quakers but country Quakers, however, made all the difference. Particularly it made the difference that John Woolman, the fourth child but eldest son of Samuel, was largely spared exposure to the conflicts and paradoxes of the Quaker historical situation until after he had absorbed its culture pure. That, and his possible exposure to the literature of "quietism," may have been one reason for the appeal to the Journalist of the word "pure." When Woolman wrote to frontier "Friends in the Back Settlements of North Carolina" thirty years after, he was clearly reflecting his sense of his own childhood environment:

And now Dear Friends and Brethren, as you are improving a wilderness, and may be numbered amongst the first planters in one part of a Province, I beseech you in the Love of Jesus Christ, to wisely consider the force of your Examples, and think how much your successors may be thereby affected. It is a help in a Country, yea, a great favor and a blessing, when Customs first settled are agreeable to sound wisdom, so, when they are otherwise, the Effect of them is grievous, and children find themselves encompassed with difficulties

prepared for them by their predecessors. . . .
The works of Righteousness are peace, and the
Effects of Righteousness are quietness and as-
surance forever.

Dwell here, my Dear Friends; and then in
Remote and Solitary Deserts, you may find
true peace and satisfaction.

In his religious response to the force of that
culture he was not unique, he was traditional. In
the formal purity of his religious experience, faithful to its ancestry, and in the shaping power of his
expressive imagination originated his significance
as John Woolman.

Chapter III

WOOLMAN'S QUAKERISM

I had a Dream about the ninth year of my age as follows: I saw the Moon rise near the West, and run a regular course Eastward, so swift that in about a quarter of an hour, she reached our Meridian, when there descended from her a small Cloud on a Direct line to the Earth, which lighted on a pleasant Green about twenty yards from the Door of my Father's House (in which I thought I stood) and was immediately turned into a beautiful green Tree. The Moon appeared to run on with Equal swiftness, and soon set in the East, at which time the Sun arose at the place where it commonly doth in the Summer, and Shining with full Radiance in a Serene air, it appeared as pleasant a morning as ever I saw.

All this time I stood in the door, in an Awful frame of mind, and I observed that as heat increased by the Rising Sun, it wrought so powerfully on the little green Tree, that the leaves gradually withered, and before Noon it appeared dry and dead. Then there appeared a Being, Small of Size, moving Swift from the North Southward, called a *"Sun Worm."*

Though I was A Child, this dream was instructive to me.

The boy's "Sun Worm" dream must have been vivid indeed—or, what is likelier, repeated—for it to have stayed so sharply in his memory. Just how it was "instructive" to him, what it said, he never told; and it would be presumptuous to pretend to interpret it now. It and Woolman's other intense dreams and visions were suppressed from the printed *Journal* for more than a century and a half, and most of his readers, now as always, read piously bowdlerized text. What the visions tell us unmistakably is that John Woolman's religious life was psychically more striking and mystically more explicit than has been generally supposed.

The mystic's claim is experiential and therefore irreducible. One may accept it, reject it, or undertake to explain it away. One may screen or classify or systematize it according to categorical patterns of phenomena. It remains stubbornly personal, a fact of individual experience. When all is said, perhaps it is best to define the mystic occurrence as an experienced encounter of the human with the divine. Then, if one supposes such an encounter to be possible on any terms, it seems probable that the standing Quaker question is whether that experience has taken place with a transcendent God, the "Wholly Other," or with an immanent God Within the normal processes of man and nature.

The Quaker tradition of the inner light would seem to permit either answer or, ambiguously, often both.[1] And so it was with John Woolman. The

---

[1] For a recent and neutral general discussion see Leif Eeg-Olofsson, *The Conception of the Inner Light in Robert Barclay's Theology: A Study in Quakerism* (Lund, Gleerup, 1954). The mystic-transcendent view was argued repeatedly at one pole by the late, great Rufus Jones; at least equally polar in arguing the immanent-to-natural view is Brand Blanshard, "Early Thought on the Inner Light," *Byways in Quaker History*, ed. H. H. Brinton (Wallingford: Pendle Hill, 1944), pp. 153–78.

fascinating fact is that with him religion which was clearly radical, absolutely individual, profoundly personal, should turn out also to be perfectly aligned to the forms, the conventions, of a tradition. He ran his race to conversion with all the agonies and joys of genuine struggle to victory. He was a man of sorrows and acquainted with despair, even horror, as well as grief. Yet one sees in those agonies and ecstasies a kind of foregone quietness of growth, the fulfillment of a natural process, a peace more than commonly Quakerly. Only the visions were unique; and they, too, as occurrences, though not in their unique content and relation to Woolman's psyche, had a place in the tradition.[2]

I

The smoothly organic voluntarism of Woolman's conversion, for instance, makes the classic Augustinian irruption of irresistible grace upon his American contemporary Jonathan Edwards seem rather garish. For all Edwards' yearning, he had to pant for grace in vain until "a wonderful alteration in [his] mind" occurred to him mysteriously.[3] Regularly trained, sensitively responsive, Woolman had only to subdue his will. Even in childhood his tenderness and responsibility of conscience came out when, idly stoning a mother robin, he hit and killed her. Aghast, he realized that the baby birds would now starve to death and he must climb the tree and give them a merciful death. Doing it, he thought Scrip-

[2] See Howard H. Brinton, "Dreams of Quaker Journalists," *Byways in Quaker History*, pp. 209–31; F. B. Tolles, "The Dream of John Woolman," *American Friends Service Committee Bulletin*, October, 1951, pp. 19–20.

[3] "Personal Narrative," *Jonathan Edwards*, Faust and Johnson, eds. (New York: American Book Co., 1935), p. 59.

ture fulfilled in himself: "The tender mercies of the wicked are Cruel." Thereafter the sensitivity of his identification with animals became extraordinary.

On the whole, however, Woolman was hard put to it to scrape up enough sin to justify a real repentance. At the age of sixteen he began "to love wanton company: and though I was preserved from profane language or Scandalous conduct, Still I perceived a plant in me which produced wild grapes." One gathers that he fell into the fun-loving company of frivolous Quaker young people and discovered in himself a talent for "myrth and wantonness." Repeated trials of repentance and reformation conquered this indulgence in what seem to have been the courting customs of that innocent countryside, and John Woolman "learned to bear the Cross":

I kept steady to meetings, spent firstdays in the afternoon chiefly in reading the scriptures and other good Books, and was early convinced in my mind that true Religion consisted in an inward life, wherein the Heart doth Love and Reverence God the Creator, and learn to Exercise true Justice and Goodness, not only toward all men, but also toward the Brute Creatures. That as the mind was moved by an inward Principle to Love God as an invisible, Incomprehensible Being, by the same principle it was moved to love him in all his manifestations in the Visible world. That as by his breath the flame of life was kindled in all Animal and Sensible Creatures, to say we Love God as unseen, and at the same time Exercise cruelty toward the least creature moving by his life, or by life derived from Him, was a Contradiction in itself.[4]

From that moment he could devote his life to becoming a thorough Quaker—or, as he saw it, a true Christian. For, as Woolman said in this context and in a famous sentence: "I found no narrowness respecting Sects and Opinions, but believe that sincere upright-hearted people, in Every society that truly love God are accepted of HIM." Thus from his nineteenth into his twenty-first year Woolman lived at home and cultivated in secret an experience he found incommunicable except by hints to those who had also known it: ". . . an awfullness covered me: my heart was tender and often contrite, and a universal Love to my fellow Creatures increased in me." He could only suggest how to glimpse it in others. "Some glances of Real beauty are perceivable in their faces, who dwell in true meekness, Some tincture of true Harmony in the sound of that voice to which Divine Love gives utterance, and Some appearance of right order in their temper and Conduct, whose passions are fully regulated. . . ." But one had to know to see.

---

[4] That Woolman's conversion fell well within the Quaker tradition (though perhaps toward its milder pole because of the historical ascendancy of his culture) is indicated by Luella M. Wright's observation of four stock elements throughout the journals: (1) accepting the Light; (2) accepting Quaker practice; (3) acquiring peace; (4) entering upon the ministry and sufferings (*The Literary Life of the Early Friends, 1650–1725* [New York: Columbia University Press, 1932], p. 193). Brinton sees in the journals of three centuries "the spiritual journey . . . in three main stages": childhood, with primitive innocence and intimations of divine love and grace; adolescence, with juvenile frivolity, conflict, and struggle; the mature breakthrough of "complete willingness to follow the Light Within" (*Friends for 300 Years*, p. 206).

II

Usually, it may be suspected, for romantic reasons, Woolman commentators have underscored the paradox of his writing's having come from an "illiterate," "unlearned," poverty-stricken "tailor" or "shopkeeper." Of course, such things are relative, and Woolman was neither a scholar nor an intellectual. He was no Cotton Mather, no James Logan; the intellectual drive and brilliance of an Edwards would have seemed abhorrent to Woolman. Quaker anti-intellectualism aside, however, he seems to have known that he had to prepare himself; and he intimates that he now began to read as he could: ". . . having had schooling pretty well for a planter, I used to improve winter evenings, and other leisure times. . . ."

And that raises the vexing but interesting question of what Woolman read. For actual evidence of his reading there exist reference, quotation, and allusion in his writings and a tiny list of twenty-eight "books lent" from his personal library to friends, and recorded in his ledger.[5] On the sound assumption that Woolman read his own books, this list extends the knowledge of his reading to be gleaned from citations in his writings to something in the neighborhood of forty separate volumes.

Predictably, the bulk of these works is Quaker. Four are Quaker "classics": Fox's *Book of Doctrinals,* Barclay's *Apology,* Sewel's *History,* and Penn's *No Cross No Crown.* No less than nine are the testi-

---

[5] See F. B. Tolles, "John Woolman's List of 'Books Lent,'" *Bulletin of Friends Historical Association,* XXXI (Autumn, 1942), pp. 72–81; also Walter Altman, "John Woolman's Reading" (unpub. diss., Florida State University, 1957).

monies or "journals" on which Woolman modeled himself—those of John Churchman (read in MS), William Dewsbury, John Fothergill, John Gratton, Frances Howgill, Gilbert Latey, Humphrey Smith, Elizabeth Stirredge, Thomas Story, and Thomas Wilson. *Polemics,* a volume of verse by Mary Mollineux, and an unidentifiable collection of "devotional tracts" complete the list.

Predictably again, the bulk of the rest is religious. John Foxe's *Acts and Monuments* (or *Book of Martyrs*) and William Cave's *Primitive Christianity: or the Religion of the Ancient Christians in the First Ages of the Gospel* were obviously useful to Woolman. Less predictable were Dodsley, *The Oeconomy of Human Life* and William Sherlock, *A Practical Discourse Concerning Death.* A startling glance, however fatally dull the art, toward the eighteenth-century world of intellectual cultivation was Sir Richard Blackmore's reply to Lucretius: *Creation, A Philosophical Poem, in Seven Books.*

The practical Woolman had books on navigation (and surveying?), cider making, and Indian treaties, *Every Man His Own Lawyer,* and a "Merchant's Pocket Book." Another startling leap toward current intellectual sophistication was John Locke, philosopher-psychologist of the age, with a book not yet popular in the colonies, *Some Thoughts Concerning Education.* There was also, quite naturally, a group of travels, histories, geography, and polemic associated with slavery. Finally, Woolman knew a block of books connecting his own experience with the mystic traditions of Europe: Thomas à Kempis, the anonymous *Desiderius, or the Original Pilgrim,* Jakob Boehme, Dr. John Everard, and William Law.

From these, as from much of Woolman's reading,

it would be easy to extrapolate and prove too much or too little. Obviously Woolman read more than this. Nobody lends out all his books, nobody cites all his reading. To take an obvious example, it is inconceivable that Woolman had not read the journal of George Fox. He is known to have had a well-stocked library available at John Smith's in Burlington. On the basis of this reading and its implications (if only from Woolman's skillful handling of it in writing) one can dismiss the notions that he was "illiterate," or "uneducated," or "a cultural primitive." He was none of these, but a literate cultural provincial—as every contemporary American had to be at best—with special reading interests. He was sophisticated enough to marshal ideas and control style to his ends—quite literate enough, in short, to have created in his *Journal* a work of literary art—without the intervention of any forces more miraculous than those of his own heart, mind, and imagination.

Having checked the romantic temptation to portray Woolman as a spontaneous, primitive cultural mutation, one is left uneasily with the opposite temptation to interpret him as a hidden scholar, a Quaker Faust. But obviously nothing of the kind was true. Woolman's learning was probably much more like Walt Whitman's, of the patchy, derivative, self-educated, provincial, and poetic sort. *No Cross No Crown,* Everard's book, and Cave's *Primitive Christianity* were in part compendia. Had Woolman, in referring to Eusebius and Polycarp, read them himself or picked them up secondarily? It would have been like a Quaker pragmatist, like an early American and an enthusiast, to adopt the Emersonian practice of reading only with the ideal of finding in a book what was there for oneself. Why go further? It seems likely that Woolman did not.[6] On the other hand, there is almost surely a body of reading behind Woolman's thought that was hidden (in the sense of never acknowledged, never alluded to, perhaps because it was "head knowledge"). That was in the natural-rights philosophies of the great European Enlightenment in full sway in Woolman's time. As we shall see, he used their thought with the ease of assimilation. Had he read Milton or Sidney, Locke on government as well as education, perhaps even Shaftesbury? We shall probably never know.

On the other hand, there can be no doubt about John Woolman's command of the Bible. His use of it was easy, allusive, and cogent. He quoted frequently and with an intimate familiarity which showed that he *thought* biblically. That same readiness frequently led him into careless, insignificant errors in matters which he seems never to have supposed it necessary to check. He cites the Bible perhaps four hundred times in writing, quoting obscure texts readily, but concentrating on familiar ones, and often strategically identifying himself or his reader

---

[6] This likelihood seems to me to bear against Dr. Altman's conviction that he can show "that mystical tradition was a major influence at work upon [Woolman's] consciousness" (p. 2); if he means, as he appears to, a bookish tradition of "the quietist strain of mysticism which developed in Roman Catholic thought during the Counter-Reformation, spread to Italy, Spain, and France by the seventeenth century and affected the outlook of the Quakers in the eighteenth" (p. 24), the case is "not proven"; there just isn't enough evidence. The same trouble, complicated by an inherent flaw in the method of proof, applies to the efforts of Amelia Mott Gummere and Rufus Jones to prove French quietist influence, specifically that of Mme. Guyon, Fénelon, and Molinos, on Woolman. No documentary evidence appears. And efforts to prove influence by occasional similarity of phrase or simply by the evidence of one's inner stylistic ear are so notoriously unreliable as to have been abandoned in professional literary studies. (Cp. Amelia Mott Gummere, ed., "Introduction," *The Journal and Essays of John Woolman* (New York: The Macmillan Co., 1922), p. 15; and Jones, "Evidences of the Influence of Quietism on John Woolman," *Friends Intelligencer*, V (March 6, 1948), pp. 131–2.

with a scriptural situation or personage. He divides his attention fairly evenly between the Old and New Testaments, with the Gospels according to Matthew and John dominating the latter, and the major prophets, overwhelmingly Isaiah and Jeremiah, the former. Favorite passages are the Lord's Prayer, the Golden Rule, and, not surprisingly, the tandem of "Lay not up for yourselves treasures upon earth . . ." (Matthew 6:19) and ". . . your life is hid with Christ in God" (Colossians 3:3). The significant evidence, however, is that, in the light of his special context, Woolman's mental life was biblical.[7]

II

With chronological manhood came John Woolman's decision upon a way of life. Apparently he had recognized for some time that hand-labor farming was physically too taxing and that his would have to be the way of a clerk, or perhaps a craftsman, in his culture. That decision necessitated village life, and so in 1741 he moved into nearby Mount Holly "to tend Shop and keep books" for "a man in much business at Shopkeeping and Baking." Eventually, though he succeeded as a young village factotum, Woolman swallowed some pride and learned "the Taylor's trade," in the belief that he was led to his humility by "Providence" and "Expecting that if I should settle I might by this trade and a little retailing of goods get a living in a plain way without the load of great business."

If, as seems likely, what humility and the inner light were denying to John Woolman was the

---

[7] I am particularly indebted to Prof. Alison Ensor for analyses of Woolman's use of the Bible, studies that I hope will eventually find separate publication.

Quaker way to wealth so brilliantly mastered by
Benjamin Franklin, Woolman's religious compen-
sations were correspondingly great. Not that he
entered upon poverty—"competence" was the eighteenth-century word for it, the ability to stand solidly on your own financial feet, to defy the taunt of
Poor Richard: "It is hard for an empty bag to stand
upright." There was a quiet pride in his totaling up
his income from tailoring alone in his ledger for the
first year, 1743–44, as £20 4s. 5d. Nor was that income only a base for "plain living"; by 1747 he was
buying property in Mount Holly.

But this was mere "competence" in the overt
world of men. Internally, and for long in secret,
priceless gains were made. Eventually he crossed a
threshold by rising to speak in the Mount Holly
Meeting, shamed himself into sore affliction by
saying "more than was required of me," recovered
his poise six weeks later, and spoke "the language
of the pure Spirit which inwardly moves upon the
heart. . . ." Thence he grew swiftly into "the
publick ministry" of his sect. His account of what
was happening was characteristically deeply Quaker
and unsectarian:

> The outward modes of worship are various,
> but wheresoever men are true Ministers of
> Jesus Christ, it is from the operation of his
> Spirit upon their hearts . . . giving them a feel-
> ing sense of the conditions of others. This
> truth was early fixed in my mind, and I was
> taught to watch the pure opening, and to take
> heed lest while I was standing to speak, my
> own will should get uppermost, and cause me
> to utter words from worldly wisdom, and de-

part from the channel of the true Gospel
Ministry.

On August 27, 1743, the Burlington Quarterly
Meeting of Ministers and Elders entered a minute
accepting him into "unity" as a member. He was
still twenty-two years old and had become a "publick minister." Some view of the context and ethos
of that ministry may be gathered from certain observations by a none too sympathetic visitor to
Philadelphia in 1749. As Peter Kalm, a Swedish
Finn, saw them:

The Quakers in this town attend meeting
three times every Sunday from ten to twelve
in the morning, at two in the afternoon, and
finally at six in the evening. Besides, they attend
service twice during the week, namely on Tues-
days from ten to twelve and on Thursdays at
the same time. Then also a religious service is
held in the church the last Friday of each
month, not to mention their general gatherings,
which I shall discuss presently. —Today people
appeared at ten, as the bells of the English
church were ringing. We sat down on benches
made like those in our academies on which the
students sit. The front benches, however, were
provided with a long, horizontal pole in the
back, against which one could lean for support.
Men and Women sit apart. (In London, they
sat together.) The early comers sit on the front
seats, and so on down. Nearest the front by the
walls are two benches, one on either side of
the aisle, made of boards like our ordinary
pews, and placed a little higher up than the
other seats in the church. On one of them, on

the men's side, sat today two old men; on the other, in the women's section, were four women. In these pews sit those of both sexes who either are already accustomed to preach or who expect on that particular day to be inspired by the Holy Ghost to expound the Word. . . . When a man comes into the meeting-house he does not remove or raise his hat but goes and sits down with his hat on.

Here we sat and waited very quietly from ten o'clock to a quarter after eleven, during which the people gathered and then waited for inspiration of the Spirit to speak. Finally, one of the two aforementioned old men in the front pew rose, removed his hat, turned hither and yon, and began to speak, but so softly that even in the middle of the church, which was not very large, it was impossible to hear anything except the confused murmur of the words. Later he began to talk a little louder, but so slowly that four or five minutes elapsed between the sentences; finally the words came both louder and faster. In their preaching the Quakers have a peculiar mode of expression, which is half singing, with a strange cadence and accent, and ending each cadence, as it were, with a half or occasionally a full sob. Each cadence consists of two, three or four syllables, but sometimes more, according to the demand of the words and meaning; e.g., my friends/ / put in your mind/ / we can/ / do nothing/ / good of our selves/ / without God's/ / help and assistance/ / etc. In the beginning the sobbing is not heard so plainly, but the deeper and further the speaker gets into his sermon the stronger becomes the sobbing between the cadences. The speaker to-day made no gestures, but turned in various directions; occasionally he placed one hand on his cheek; and during most of the sermon kept buttoning and unbuttoning his vest with his right hand. The gist of his sermon was that we can do nothing good of ourselves without the help and support of our Savior. When he had stood for a while using his sing-song method he changed his manner of delivery and spoke in a more natural way, or as our ministers do when they say a prayer. Shortly afterwards, however, he began again his half-singing mode of expression and at the end, just as he was speaking at his best, he stopped abruptly, sat down and put on his hat. . . .

The meeting-house was whitewashed inside and had a gallery almost all the way around. The tin candle-holders on the pillars supporting the gallery constituted the only ornaments of the church. There was no pulpit, altar, baptismal font, or bridal pew, no priedieu nor collection bag, no clergyman, cantor nor church beadle, and no announcements were made after the sermon, nor were any prayers said for the sick. This was the way the service was conducted today.

But now I shall describe how it was often conducted otherwise. Many times after a long silence a man preaches first, and when he gets through a woman rises and preaches; and after her comes another man or woman; occasionally only the women speak; then again a woman might be the first, and so on alternately; sometimes only men rise to talk; now and then either a man or woman gets up, begins to puff and sigh, and endeavors to speak, but is unable to squeeze out a word and so sits down again. Then it happens, also, that the whole congregation gathers in the meeting-house and sits there silently for two hours, waiting for someone to preach; but since none has prepared himself or as they say feels moved by the Holy Spirit, the whole audience rises again at the end of the period and goes home without the members having accomplished anything in the church except sit there and look at each other. . . .[8]

Though obviously cold, as the notations of the representative of an aristocratic established church upon the strange doings of an enthusiastic and leveling sect, testimony like Kalm's, of a detached and largely disinterested observer, is worth volumes of partisan or synthetic portraiture. And one of its most striking features is its registration of classic Quakerism's usual, even institutionalized emotionality. The closest thing to it in our own time is perhaps the fervency of the religion of the "store-front" churches. Quakerism, says Brinton, was in the beginning a "group mysticism," and "the presence of the Light of Christ enabled the meeting to become the Body of Christ . . ." and in that process, individuals and groups dissolved, frequently "melting into tears." [9]

As a renewer of his tradition, a kind of neo-primitive Friend, John Woolman in his "tenderness" seems to have "melted" habitually. His *Journal's* coolness of tone and limpidity of style were the re-

[8] Henry J. Cadbury, "Philadelphia Quakerism in 1749 as Seen by a Finn," *Bulletin of the Friends Historical Association,* XXXI (Spring, 1942), pp. 28–30.

[9] *Friends for 300 Years,* pp. xiv, 4, 14.

sult of a successful discipline of mind and expression. But beneath the discipline burned the fires of a powerfully emotional heart (as in his weepings and openings) and an explosively passionate preconscious imagination (as in his potent dreams).

Such experiences and their free expression were natural to Woolman, and it is important to the understanding of the man and his work that his readers not forget or ignore the facts. One hesitates to suggest that he used such "tenderness" as a weapon. He was simply accustomed to it as a personally genuine event—however formalized it was becoming in his Society—and there is testimony both in the *Journal* and outside it that he sometimes, with whatever motivation, employed it strategically. Where in another generation pugnacious Elias Hicks split the Society wide apart, Woolman moved it effectively through humility. As an ancient eyewitness testified, one of the hardest places for Woolman to convict against slavery was Mount Holly, his own Nazareth. When he first began to speak against slavery there

. . . he was often publicly opposed. When that was the case he would sit down & weep without attempting any justification. In the course of a few years his concern found a place in the minds of his friends Generally & the Society was enabled to wash their hands from the Guilt of slave holding.[10]

Though to our desperately antisentimental age such emotionality makes Woolman less available, it may actually have made him more honestly hu-

[10] John Cox, "Sketches and Recollections of Prominent Friends and Historic Facts" (MS, Historical Society of Pennsylvania), p. 1.

man than we (for what do we dare weep?). And
certainly it made him, in all but a few exalted
circles, more available to his own age. It helped in
the merely personal aspects of his ministry. In
face-to-face dealings he seems to have been defended from the dryness, the canny, even astringent
reserve in human relations behind which Quaker
notions of love are often concealed. His neighbor
heard ". . . a peculiar melody in his voice. He was
a peace maker in his neighborhood and skillful in
reconciling differences." [11] Nor did this make him
owlish. Mount Holly cherished a few tiny ancedotes
to prove that his youthful humor survived, however
chastened.[12]

Woolman's "publick" yet nonprofessional ministry,
thus, had three aspects: a pastoral responsibility
for the individual well-being of his neighbors; a
parochial responsibility for his community; and
the unlimited responsibilities of the "traveling
Friend." At the very outset of his ministry he found
it necessary to exert his parochial responsibility:

> About the time called Christmas I observed
> many people from the Country, and dwellers in
> Town, who resorting to publick houses, spent
> their time in drinking and vain sports, tending
> to corrupt one another, on which account I was
> much troubled. At one house in particular
> there was much disorder, and I believed it was
> a duty laid on me to go and speak to the
> master of that house. I considered I was young,
> and that several Elderly friends in Town had
> opportunity to See these things, and though I

[11] *Ibid.*, p. 25.
[12] *Ibid.*, p. 1.

would gladly have been excused, yet I could not feel my mind clear. The Exercise was heavy, and as I was Reading what the Almighty Said to Ezekiel, respecting his duty as a watchman, the matter was set home more clearly, and then with prayer and tears, I besought the Lord for his Assistance, who in loving kindness gave me a Resigned heart. Then at a suitable Opportunity, I went to the publick house, and Seeing the man amongst a company, I went to him and told him I wanted to speak with him. So we went aside, and there in the Fear and dread of the Almighty I Exprest to him what rested on my mind, which he took kindly, and afterward showed more regard to me than before. In a few years, after he died, middle-aged, I often thought that had I neglected my duty in that case, it would have given me great trouble and I was humbly thankful to my Gracious Father, who had supported me therein.

III

Very swiftly, however, John Woolman found his true calling in the "traveling ministry." As Janet Whitney has said eloquently, "The Religious Society of Friends depends in an extraordinary way on person to person influence. It has no pope, no bishop, no moderator, no head executive . . . body. . . . But in each generation traveling Friends . . . arise, who by personal magnetism, a contagious faith, and a devotion to an occasional, voluntary, itinerant ministry, act as a living cement to fix the whole Society together. . . ." [13]

[13] "Rufus Jones: Friend," *The Atlantic Monthly,* 193 (April, 1954), p. 29.

From the earliest "Publishers of Truth" the Quakers had progressed that way. George Fox himself had visited America. Burlington, as we have seen, had profited richly from visitation. And in Woolman's critical nineteenth year, New Jersey had been harrowed by the famous independent evangelist, George Whitefield, in one episode of the famous Great Awakening. It was no wonder that in the fall of 1743 Woolman should join his "Esteemed Friend Abraham Farrington . . . to make a Visit to Friends on the Eastern side of this Province. . . ."

For a period thereafter Woolman found his vocation as a traveler wide-ranging indeed. He seems to have become at once an apostle to the Quakers struggling to survive in the nascent nation and an explorer of his country. Few if any men knew provincial America more extensively or, excepting Woolman's limitation to Quakerly concerns, more intimately than he. He journeyed from North Carolina in the South to Massachusetts in the North, from forest frontiers to tidelands and out to Nantucket at sea. By the computations of the *Journal*, in 1746–48 he covered 2,390 American miles in the saddle and 150 under sail. In the course of it all he discovered a major duty—to tend the scattered sheep of his own Society—and a concern which would govern all the rest of his life. The black men and women in bondage in America must be freed; and first the Quakers must be freed of the guilt of oppressing any of them.

Chapter IV

SLAVERY AND THE CRISIS OF 1755

Two things were remarkable to me in this journey. First, in regard to my Entertainment. When I eat, drank and lodged free-cost with people who lived in Ease on the hard toil of their slaves I felt uneasy, and as my mind was inward to the Lord, I found, from place to place, this uneasiness return upon me. . . . Where the masters bore a good deal of the burthen and lived frugally, so that their Servants were well provided for, and their labour moderate, I felt more easy; but where they lived in a costly way, and laid heavy burthens on their Slaves, my exercise was often great, and I frequently had conversation with them in private concerning it. Secondly, This trade of importing Slaves . . . being much Encouraged . . . I saw in these Southern Provinces, so many Vices and Corruptions increased by this trade and this way of life, that it appeared to me as a dark gloominess hanging over the Land, and . . . in future the Consequence will be grievous to posterity. I express it as it hath appeared to me, not at once, or twice, but as a matter fixed on my mind.

In retrospect it is not easy to say why the Quakers

responded so slowly to the challenge of human slavery. There was no fully formed Quaker position on the subject until John Woolman formed it a century after Fox had begun his work. To achieve this was one of Woolman's two major creative acts, and it is doubtless one of the principal evidences for the contention that his age was truly one of Quaker creativity. Perhaps the Quaker slowness in this regard tells us things of importance about the nature of the challenges of the colonial American situation, as well as things about the modes and possibilities of human response to moral elements in cultural challenge.

In the English colonies, the white colonists' reactions to Negro slaves appear to have been Calvinistic or Hobbesian when they were not merely mercenary, aggressive, culture-bound, or even sadistic. It was not only a racial matter: seventeenth-century colonists were accustomed to bound apprentices, indentured servants, transported criminals, and whites as well as Indians sold into slavery for political or other reasons. As Quakers had ample reason to know, it was a callous age throughout the world. Its barter in flesh could be defended as more humane than its remnants of judicial torture, its murderous prisons, its common personal brutality, its public scarifyings, scourgings, brandings, mutilations, hangings, and burnings.

Not only the pathos of Quaker experience with persecution (which had brought many of them overseas) but the genius of their religion militated against such views and ways. The "Holy Experiment" and all its kindred abolished from the beginning the pain- and horror-filled, the bloody habits of an unenlightened past. They kept the institutions of apprenticeship and indenture as disciplinary, responsible traditions of mutual benefit to master and servant. But such had definite terms and, certainly for serious Quakers, no brutality. How then, as from the earliest dates they obviously did, were they able to adopt the Caribbean and American system of keeping Negro slaves?

One part of the answer seems to be that they succumbed to overwhelming economic temptation. The most familiar fact about a frontier is that it blots up manpower insatiably. And in slavery, manpower was available as if it came from horses or oxen—domestic stock. Another part appears to be that the Quakers (and for long after John Woolman) were, like everyone else, unable to solve the cross-cultural problem. The Negroes were not only black and strange, they were "savage." Still more baffling, they came stripped of their own culture and context, "raw" from the slaver. Or else, as chattels, they found English (or Quaker) culture walled away, and slave culture, never to be adequate, still a-borning. The resultant difficulties of communication perhaps made it hard to tell whether Negro slaves really had the Light Within, whether, in short, they were really human. Perhaps the margin of doubt left room for the temptations to quicker, larger wealth which Woolman exposed to condemnation in slaveholding Friends and room for that sin even worse, the exercise of absolute power over other human beings.

I

To say such things is not to intimate that the Quakers were insensitive to slavery from the start: the reverse is of course true; it is only to speculate on how there came to be a problem for the creative conscience of John Woolman. The history of American Quaker involvement with slavery has been definitively told by Thomas E. Drake, who sums up the early experience: "The only significant movement against slavery in colonial America took place among the Quakers. They too groped their way slowly, with heart searching, toward the conviction that slavery could not truly be reconciled with their Christian faith." [1] It was that generations-long slowness which kindled Woolman.

From the beginning George Fox had been concerned, and he wrote as early as 1657 "To Friends Beyond Sea, that Have Blacks and Indian Slaves" to caution them to the mercifulness of Christ and the necessity to bring His "glad tidings to every captivated creature under the whole heaven." In Barbados in 1671 Fox sowed the seeds of abolition by preaching to slaves and urging their owners to set an indenture-like term to their servitude. The efforts of Quakers to follow even parts of his injunction aroused such persecution on the sugar-rich island that Quakerism was shortly almost stamped out. In that still-prophetic period, the resultant conflict raised in William Edmundson the first true abolitionist. He was followed in 1688 by a group of German Quakers who queried their monthly meeting, and through it the Philadelphia

---

[1] *Quakers and Slavery in America* (New Haven: Yale University Press, 1950), p. 4. Much of the succeeding historical summation rests on Drake.

Quarterly and Yearly Meetings, with embarrassing questions about slavery: Could it fulfill the Golden Rule? Did it make Christians any better than Turks? Was it not a complex of crimes? How could it be reconciled with Quaker testimonies of love, peace, liberty, and nonviolence? Still more embarrassing was a 1693 pamphlet from the Keithian schismatic "Christian Quakers," called "An Exhortation & Caution to Friends Concerning Buying or Keeping of Negroes."

The first reactions of official Quakerdom on both sides of the Atlantic to these protests amounted to an embarrassed silence under cover of which Quaker slavery flourished. In another wealthier and worldlier generation, conservatives could feel that they had gone as far as they needed by condemning actual participation in the African slave trade. They used the growing disciplinary powers of the committees they ruled to silence and, if necessary, to excommunicate critics of slaveholding. It became dangerous to a good Friend to attack slavery. Prevailing slaveowners thought it disownably disorderly and threatening to the "unity" of the Society. They achieved silence if not unity for a decade until in 1729 Ralph Sandiford and, shortly afterward, Benjamin Lay raised prophetic voices, defied the "grandees," were duly expelled, and scandalized the Quaker culture.

Especially Benjamin Lay scandalized it. Though there may never be definitive evidence to prove it, it is probable that Lay impressed John Woolman profoundly, and eventually, perhaps, haunted him. Lay was of the antique prophetic Quaker breed, God-intoxicated and extravagant in his testimonies, implacable, unswervable, explosively imaginative in propaganda—the sort of Quaker who had exas-

perated the authorities of Old and New England
to persecution and even in the mildness of the
Quaker culture became intolerable. A hunchback,
Lay lived in a cave, bore testimonies for vegetarian-
ism and against the use of animal wool as well as
tobacco and the drinking of tea and alcohol. But
his principal target was the slavery which had
agonized him until he fled Barbados in 1731, and
which he found unbearably hypocritical in the land
of the Friends.

Lay's thesis and attitude are clearly set forth in
the title of the book he brought, pages scrambled
in a prophetic disdain, for printing to Benjamin
Franklin—who sympathetically did his best for it
and cannily left his name off the title page:

*All Slave-Keepers, That keep the Innocent in
Bondage, Apostates Pretending to lay claim
to the Pure & Holy Christian Religion; of
what Congregation soever; but especially in
their Ministers, by whose example the filthy
Leprosy and Apostasy is spread far and near;
it is a notorious Sin, which many of the true
friends of Christ, and his pure Truth, called
Quakers, has been for many Years, and still are
concern'd to write and bear Testimony against;
as a Practice so gross & hurtful to Religion,
and destructive to Government, beyond what
Words can set forth, or can be declared by Men
or Angels, and yet lived in by Ministers and
Magistrates in America. The Leaders of the
People cause them to Err. Written for a General Service, by him that truly and sincerely
desires the present and eternal Welfare and
Happiness of all Mankind, all the World over,*

of all Colours, and Nations, as his own Soul.
(1737)

It is unimaginable that Woolman should not have known of Lay. Lay had been disowned privately for notoriously effective stunts in dramatizing his obsession, but in 1730 the Yearly Meeting took the ultimate step of publicly disowning him. That same year, when the Yearly Meeting met in Burlington and young John Woolman, on the threshold of his full conversion, was almost surely there, Lay staged his most famous demonstration. He rose in the silence, draped in a Quaker coat and holding what appeared to be a Bible in his hand. "Oh, all you Negro masters," he proclaimed, ". . . you might as well throw off the plain coat as I do"—and threw it back theatrically to reveal himself, in that drab audience wholly unaccustomed to dramatics, in military regalia including a sword. And he was not done. "It would be as justifiable in the sight of the Almighty," he continued, "if you should thrust a sword through their hearts as I do through this book." Then he drew his sword, plunged it into his hollowed-out book, which hid a bladder of red liquid (perhaps pokeberry juice), and squirted the "blood" over the shocked faces and swooning women around him.[2]

Of course, they threw Benjamin Lay out of the house as they had from the Society. But that neither confuted him nor diminished his life-likeness to the prophetic and not seldom outrageous first Friends. How much Lay became an inspiration and how much he served as a warning to John Woolman no one can really tell. The Woolmans had never kept

---

[2] Of the many accounts of Lay, the most useful is that of Drake, pp. 43–7, 221.

slaves, and Samuel Woolman had "all along been
deeply Affected with the Oppression of the poor
Negroes . . ." (though John Woolman's maternal
grandfather was a slaveholder).[3] Something, at any
rate, at the crucial time of Woolman's entry upon
the ministry, made him "uneasy" at being directed
by his employer to draft a bill of sale for a Negro
woman the employer was selling off:

> . . . yet I remembered I was hired by the year;
> that it was my master who directed me to do
> it, and that it was an Elderly man, a member of
> our society who bought her, so through weak-
> ness I gave way . . . but at the Executing it I
> was so Affected in my mind, that I said before
> my Master and the Friend, that I believed slave-
> keeping to be a practice inconsistent with the
> Christian Religion. . . .

It was a troubled young radical who rode the long
miles, especially in the South, inspecting the Quaker
practice of slavery as he meditated, preached, and
conversed. By 1746 he had written at least a draft
of a radical document, not to be published for seven
years, utterly different in tone, strategy, and effect
from Benjamin Lay's, but to exactly the same point.
Two of these years he took to travel and fulfill his
earliest mission. The rest were spent in settling himself for his life's work and, at the end, launching
triumphantly upon it.

In any significantly creative life there are always
the two crucial stages: the discovery of the fundamental insights—the vision, the idea, the sense of
the possibility of form, or whatever it is; then, the
establishment of a way of life which will permit the

---

[3] Janet Whitney, *John Woolman, American Quaker* (Boston: Little,
Brown and Co., 1942), p. 102.

realization of possibility. Unlike the great failures, Woolman found his way. His Walden was to be a little orchard farm, with snug Quaker house and wife (who could let him go away in the same spirit of love and concern in which he went) and child, and a town in which to be a well-loved citizen. Woolman seems to have perceived that if he were to do his work it could not be from the eccentricity of a Benjamin Lay. However radical in reality, he needed to be a man and a brother, a citizen and householder reconciled to his culture, a man of "competence" if not substance, and from such a position he could fulfill his missions for the Friend and the slave.

II

Woolman had bought a shop in Mount Holly and eleven acres for a homestead outside the town in 1747. Now, in 1749, he took up his tailoring again, served his townsmen as surveyor, conveyancer, business agent, sometimes even as leech, and discovered that he had a talent for merchandising. He prospered, and, prospering, he took a wife. Almost, as Mrs. Whitney has remarked, as if it were a bashful afterthought, he recorded in the *Journal:*

> About this time believing it good for me to settle and thinking seriously about a Companion, my heart was turned to the Lord with desires that He would give me Wisdom to proceed therein agreeable to His Will, and he was pleased to give me a well inclined Damsel, Sarah Ellis, to whom I was married the 18 day, 8 month, 1749.[4]

---

[4] Until the calendar reform of 1752 the "first" month was March; thus, Woolman was married on October 18, 1749.

Aside from the facts which the few surviving records indicate, that theirs was a happily successful marriage and that Sarah was "well inclined" to John's religious depths as well as conjugally, we really do not know much about their marriage. A daughter, Mary, who survived, was born on December 18, 1750; and a son, William, lived only two months after birth in 1754. Neither is mentioned in the *Journal*.

Despite scrupulous shopkeeping, Woolman the businessman threatened to get rich. He came upon the paradox of what has been called "the Protestant ethic," whereby he who would do good does well. And there Woolman found himself in genuine conflict. He had a talent. He built his inventory carefully, expanded and diversified: ". . . and at length having got a considerable shop of goods, my trade increased every year, and the road to large business appeared open. . . ." After the death of his father in 1750, he had more capital. He had multiple sources of income and the taste for "a plain way of living," which Poor Richard urged so forcefully in his Almanacs, and would fix in the amber of "The Way to Wealth."

Woolman was careful to "buy and sell things really useful," not "Things that served chiefly to please the vain mind in people." He "found it good . . . to advise poor people to take such as were most useful and not costly" and not run up bills they couldn't pay. He worried about the ethics of bill collecting (though he once broke the strict Quaker code against going to law and got a warrant against a debtor he thought about to skip). He worried about the amount of rum he sold and its effects. One entry in his ledger is eloquent:

Timothy Chapman Dr. £ S. D.
8 mo. 1753

	£	S.	D.
To left unpaid for Prince		1	3
To Prince 2/1 unpaid of rum		2	4
To rum by Hamilton		1	2

I forgive this debt.

         (John Woolman)[5]

Altogether, the time came when, as the *Journal* says, "I felt a stop in my mind."

As so often, Woolman's condition was classic in the tradition of serious, or radical Quakerism. "The increase of business became my burthen," he says, "for though my natural inclination was towards merchandise, yet I believed Truth required me to live more free from outward cumbers. There was now a strife in my mind betwixt the two. . . ." Under these circumstances there was clear Quaker procedure: "and in this exercise my prayers were put to the Lord, who Graciously heard me, and gave me a heart resigned to his Holy will. . . ." And there was a traditional outcome: "I then lessened my outward business." In fact, he went out of business, phased out his merchandising and turned to freelance tailoring, orchard keeping, and conveyancy. The point is that John Woolman, once again, brought his tradition [6] to immediate vitality in his own life and thus set himself in a position to live actively, expressively, and organically the life to

---

[5] "Ledger B 1753," in Historical Society of Pennsylvania, p. 18.

[6] For the tradition see Gilbert Latey, *To all you Taylors and Brokers who lyes in Wickedness; and to all you Tradesman of what Trade, Imployment or Office soever . . .* , 1660, from which Woolman quoted in his essay "On a Sailor's Life," in Gummere, *Journal*, pp. 506–7. Cp. William C. Braithwaite, *The Second Period of Quakerism* (2nd ed.; Cambridge: Cambridge University Press, 1961), esp. pp. 499–502; Brinton, *Friends for 300 Years*, p. 138; and F. B. Tolles, *Meeting House and Counting House: The Quaker Merchants of Colonial Philadelphia, 1682–1763* (Chapel Hill: University of North Carolina Press, 1948), pp. 63–84.

which his best insights called him. He also prepared a critical viewpoint of enduring significance
to American, indeed modern, life.

Meanwhile John Woolman undertook occasional
short ministerial travels. He held fast to his quiet
testimony against any business or scribal transac-
tion having to do with slavery: "Deep rooted customs though wrong are not easily altered, but it is
the duty of every man to be firm in that which he
certainly knows is right for him." And he rose
steadily within the Society of Friends. In 1752 he
became clerk of the Burlington Quarterly Meeting
of Ministers and Elders. He was ready for his first
master strokes against the tragic evil of slavery.

III

Again, it is typical of Woolman and his *Journal*
that nothing is said in it about his rise to "weighti-
ness" and political power, or his use of that power in
the antislavery campaign. Helped not merely by his
position but by his intimacy with figures as strong in
the Yearly Meeting as Anthony Benezet, the Pembertons, and the Smiths of Burlington, Woolman
now felt ready to launch the thunderbolt he had
been readying since 1746. In 1750, his father on his
deathbed had urged John Woolman to print his
manuscript on slavery, and in 1753 he sent to the
Yearly Meeting's "overseers" of the press (of which
committee Benezet was a member) the text of
*Some Considerations on the Keeping of Negroes.
Recommended to the Professors of Christianity of
every Denomination.*

The effect was to release the Yearly Meeting
from its generation-long rigidity against the discussion of slavery. Not only did the "overseers" clear

Woolman's manuscript for publication the next year; but the Philadelphia Yearly Meeting permitted him to quote from this and other manuscripts in writing the annual "Epistle" to the Virginia Yearly Meeting in 1753; and in the year following, it accepted and had circulated to all the Quaker Yearly Meetings, American and British, as its annual communication the epoch-marking "Epistle of Caution and Advice Concerning the Buying and Keeping of Slaves" written by John Woolman.[7] After two decades, Sandiford and Benjamin Lay had in some degree been vindicated.

The two publications, little book and printed broadside, were extraordinary documents. It has usually been said that Woolman's personal saintliness made him effective. But it is worth emphasizing that if the authorship were unknown, it would still be obvious that these pieces were superbly written. The "Epistle" conforms to the necessities of its issuance. *Considerations*, however, is instantly recognizable as the work of an authentic stylist with a voice like that of no other man. Tone and substance throughout are sweetly irenic. The mind appeals only to Christian love, responsibility, and reasonableness. "My Inclination is to persuade and entreat, and simply give Hints of my Way of Thinking," says the author—who is clearly no novice but yet only in his maiden publication. He proceeds honestly by considerations, "hints," not stalking with mordant ratiocination behind a pretense of candor. He argues considerations through to conclusions rejectable by no sort of Christian. He is almost never Quaker in dogma or special phrasing; he is often

---

[7] I have accepted the convincing argument by Mrs. Whitney (pp. 193–4) that Woolman and not Anthony Benezet wrote the "Epistle" (cp. G. S. Brookes, *Friend Anthony Benezet* [Philadelphia: University of Pennsylvania Press, 1937], pp. 80–2, 475–7; Drake, p. 56).

scriptural; he works from general logic, psychology, and ethics. Not infrequently he tenders the common intellectual coin of his age: "the natural Right of Freedom"; "Nature's lawful Wants"; "a Contradiction to Reason." And he can blend the language of reason with that of Scripture to perfection:

For whosoever shall do the will of my Father which is in Heaven *(arrives at the more noble part of true relationship)* the same is my Brother, *and Sister and Mother.*

This doctrine agrees well with a state truly compleat, where LOVE *necessarily operates according* to the agreeableness of Things, on principles unalterable and in themselves perfect.

Jonathan Edwards could do no more.

Woolman was aphoristic, polished, modern for his time, and engaging. There was no way of telling from either text that he also lived a mental life occasionally opening on visions of an awful transcendency. And yet he was responsible. He made it clear to his readers, general and Quaker, that the key to the question was "the royal law," the Golden Rule, and that no plea for keeping slaves was better than inconsistent. Also, that rationalizations of such inconsistency proceeded either from self-interest or from minds perverted by the moral evils of greed or the temptations of "lording it over their Fellow Creatures, and being Masters of Men. . . ." He told his general readers "that the highest Delights of Sense, or most pleasing Objects visible, ought ever to be accounted infinitely inferior to that real intellectual Happiness suited to Man in his primitive Innocence, and now to be found in true Renovation of mind," and made it clear that such happiness could only consort with justice, equity, mercy, candor, humility, and love. He advised the Quakers to return to consistency with their historic testimonies; to face up to their individual and present as well as, in America, historic and collective sins; to get their slaves ready for freedom; and "seriously to weigh" freeing them.

These writings announced to the Quaker culture the appearance within it of a modern prophet. Like Jonathan Edwards in post-theocratic New England, here was a mind deeply given to the revival of a religious tradition but speaking the language of contemporary intellectual discourse. It would be the historic tragedy of both traditions that neither would produce an equivalent mind in the nineteenth century. Nevertheless, for the present, the specific tradition of Woolman was to be that of the Journalists, not that of Barclay, the Calvinistic Quaker theologian. Woolman's would be no Edwardsean approach toward a *Summa Theologica*. He had come to live his impulse in certain engagements with his times. Most of the writings, like these, were to be weapons in those engagements. At the end, when he was dead, the *Journal* would tell, by "hints of my way of thinking," by presenting the life as lived, what it all meant.

IV

Thus Woolman undertook to reform the Quaker culture organically from within. But, as seems always to happen, historical events crushed in upon the process of growth and altered it irrevocably. The Quaker culture entered a time of troubles from which, as a culture, it would not recover. And John Woolman, no matter what he understood consciously, apparently knew preconsciously that an apocalypse had come. On February 7, 1754, he experienced another dream vision full of cosmic imagery: two suns in the sky over his orchard; streams of fire "like a Terrible Storm coming Westward," a house full of "People with sad and troubled Aspects," and finally streams of fire standing in the sky in an inscrutable figuration:

Then there appeared on a Green plain a great Multitude of Men in a military posture, some of whom I knew: they came near the House and passing on westward, Some of them looking up at me, Exprest themselves in a Taunting way, to which I made no reply. Soon after, an old Captain of Militia came to me, and I was told that these Men were assembled to Improve in the Discipline of War.

It would be foolish to interpret this (as Woolman did not) as a kind of allegorical forecast of things to come. Yet it is tempting. For news had just appeared in Franklin's *Pennsylvania Gazette* of Washington's failure to bluff the French out of Venango and of the French determination to flank Pennsylvania down the Ohio. "All in One Year," as Robert L. D. Davidson [8] summarizes it, the Indian policies of the Quakers, of Pennsylvania, indeed of the British Empire, collapsed. Washington lost Fort Necessity, the Albany Congress got nowhere. Conrad Weiser, the dean of Pennsylvania experts, confessed: "Everything lies in such Confusion that I am quite perplexed in Mind, and do not know how to act in

[8] *War Comes to Quaker Pennsylvania, 1682–1756* (New York: Columbia University Press, 1957), pp. 113–25, 216.

Indian Affairs anymore." Next summer Major General Edward Braddock of the Coldstream Guards would be crushed and lost on the Monongahela, the Delawares would slaughter and burn on the frontiers, and the crisis of 1755 would be on.[9]

That crisis has often been discussed as if it had been simply a political matter: the pressures of real Indian and imperial war forced compromising Quaker politicians to fish or cut bait—to get out of politics or out of the Society of Friends. And that was the end of the Quaker hegemony in Pennsylvania, the end of the Friends in politics, the point of the descent of quietism upon the Society. These traditional interpretations are not wrong. But as James and Tolles suggest, the historical situation was really more complex than that. John Woolman's involvement in those complexities, the effects upon him of his involvement, and the light cast upon his thought by the crisis of 1755 are all important.

As Tolles suggests, it was a question of "The Inner Plantation and the Outer"—the souls of Quaker individuals and of their Society versus the pursuit of property and power, the stability and the health of institutions. In politics the "relativists" were ranged against the "absolutists." In the Society the "conservatives" sought to protect established accommodations against the "reformers" who sought to conserve the primitive values of the tradition by purging away the Pennsylvania compromises. Or as James puts it, "Quaker Revival" formed the base for

---

[9] The 1755 crisis in the Quaker culture merits a first-class "American Studies" sort of definitive history. Though every historian of Quakerism treats of it more or less knowledgeably, the best accounts seem to be those of Sydney V. James, *A People Among Peoples: Quaker Benevolence in Eighteenth-Century America* (Cambridge: Harvard University Press, 1963); and Tolles, *Meeting House and Counting House,* pp. 230–43, and "Quakerism and Politics," *Quakers and the Atlantic Culture* (New York: Macmillan Co., 1960), pp. 36–54.

"Coping with the Crisis of 1755." But in the clash of forces, the Quaker culture, perhaps precisely because it had been interwoven with compromise, even with what seemed to the purist "corruption," was torn apart.

Quakers had long since become a statistical minority in their tolerant Commonwealth. They had continued to control the Pennsylvania Assembly by habitual coalition with the Germans and with the anti-proprietary forces of the non-Quaker city folk led by Benjamin Franklin, naturally the most potent personality in the colony. Compromising radical Quakerism—"Pure Truth"—with the pursuit and attainment of wealth, the exercise of worldly, even military power, the "Quaker grandees" had also become past masters of political strategic obfuscation in battling with the proprietors, their royal governor, and even with London. Carefully navigating the conflicting lines of force, they had secured a larger degree of local autonomy than any other colonial legislative body.

But now, inexorably, the crisis forced them, maneuvering ever less honorably, less defensibly, toward 1756 and the end. Bound to the Quaker pacifist testimony yet determined to hold on to power, they could neither act nor, as events unfolded, refuse. In the midst of this, Woolman, joining the equally prophetic John Churchman and Anthony Benezet, and allied to the Pembertons, grasped leadership among the radicals, the reformers. For the Quarterly Meeting of Ministers and Elders in the spring of 1755, while Braddock was still preparing his catastrophe, Woolman wrote an "Epistle" sent out by the Meeting to stiffen Quakers in their pacifism: "We [who] . . . have found it to be our duty to cease from those National Contests productive of Misery and bloodshed, and submit our cause to Him the Most High . . ." addressed the Society of Friends.

By next winter, however, Woolman no longer had to depend on intuition. The frontier was naked and blazing. Franklin, almost at the end of his wits, received strategic if unexpected help from the proprietors, and the Assembly was forced at last into the passage of a militia bill (with provision for Quaker and Mennonite conscientious objection) and the passage of a revenue bill to conduct the defense of the province to the tune of sixty thousand pounds to be raised by taxes "on real and personal estates." [10] In his customarily skillful way of manipulating public opinion, Franklin published in the *Pennsylvania Gazette* for December 18 "A Dialogue between X, Y, and Z concerning the Present State of Affairs in Pennsylvania." Here he made the general conciliatory point that, while the Quakers would not fight, they and their fellow pacifists had been confirmed in this exemption from the foundation of the colony. They were good citizens and good taxpayers, and would pay where the militia were exempt.

He conciliated the warlike with a common-sense worldling's exchange at the expense of the "unco' guid":

Y: For my part I am no coward, but hang me if I'll fight to save the Quakers.
X: That is to say, You won't pump ship because 'twill save the rats, as well as yourself.

That stung the Quaker, especially the radical. But the "Dialogue" fairly represented a painful situation;

---

[10] Tolles, *Meeting House and Counting House*, p. 26.

and inherent in the situation was an accommodation which might possibly preserve the status quo of the Quaker culture. Perhaps the Quaker conservative, the grandee with his gentleman's cultivation and neatly muted conspicuous consumption, his coach in the stable, his slave in the house, and his seat in the Assembly, was as glad to see the radical stung as the door opened to accommodation. But not John Woolman.

It now became the logic of Woolman's position, as it was the resultant of his experience, that he should step to the forefront of the reformist movement. With John Churchman and the visiting Englishman, Samuel Fothergill, he moved into the prophetic, spiritual leadership. The political, activist radical banner was carried by the Pembertons, especially Israel, a gifted, forceful fighter in the "outward" means Woolman simply abandoned. To Pemberton would fall the role, already enacted by the Mathers in Boston and so often re-enacted in American history, of the radical conservative—the man of affairs with an ideal vision of the past—who seeks rather confusedly to revolutionize the present in order to conserve the values of that envisioned past. It seems not clear to what degree, in any of his roles, that figure has succeeded in turning back the hands of the historical clock.

Woolman chose to step outside, to break off, in the name of purity, the ongrowth of the cultural process—to be that kind of radical. In November he had participated in a petition to the Assembly which reminded that body of Quakers that if it passed taxes for military purposes many Quakers would "be under the necessity of suffering" rather than paying them, and Quaker magistrates would be forced to the painful historical irony of expropriating Quaker property to satisfy the demands of a Quaker-voted war tax. And on December 16, he forestalled Franklin with an "Epistle of Caution," the adoption of which split the leadership of the Society of Friends and of the Quaker culture wide open. It was the beginning of the end.

In the *Journal*, Woolman, somewhat out of chronology, as if to blunt the reader's sense of the degree of conflict involved, presents this "Epistle" in a frame of explanation. In what is apparently a constructed though historically representative discussion, Mrs. Whitney represents Churchman and Woolman as having been all along opposed to paying war taxes; but, until the crisis deepened, "With one accord Fothergill, [William] Logan, [Israel] Pemberton upheld obedience and payment." [11] And it does appear in the *Journal* that Woolman is supplying the heads of his counterargument. A Christian has to follow his own best light, regardless of what others do: Thomas à Kempis as Catholic inward reformer and John Huss as Protestant are examples. "When this exercise came upon me I knew of none under the like difficulty . . ." he said; and he went to the meetings to discuss it in considerable distress of mind.

At the meetings he would seem to have argued largely historically—directly confronting the current historical issues. Primitive Friends took "little or no" share in government but, suffering persecution "with firmness, they were made a Blessing to the Church . . . and being Afflicted by the Rulers on account of their Testimony, there was less likelihood of uniting in Spirit with them in things inconsistent

---

[11] *Op. cit.*, pp. 205–7.

with the purity of Truth." In the Quaker culture,
however, things had become altogether different:

> We, from the first settlement of this Land have
> known little or no troubles of that sort. The
> profession, which for a time was accounted re-
> proachfull, at length the uprightness of our
> predecessors being understood by the Rulers,
> and their Innocent Sufferings moving them, our
> way of Worship was tolerated, and many of
> our members in these colonies became active
> in Civil Government. Being thus tried with
> favour and prosperity, this world hath appeared
> inviting; our minds have been turned to the
> Improvement of our Country, to Merchandise
> and Sciences, amongst which are many things
> useful, being followed in pure wisdom, but in
> our present condition that a Carnal mind is
> gaining upon us I believe will not be denied.

If Quakers paid the tax, other Quakers "who are
Officers in Civil Government" might think themselves authorized to "quench the tender movings of
the Holy Spirit in their minds, and thus by small
degrees there might be an approach toward that of
Fighting" until (with razor-sharp, quiet irony) "the
distinction would be little else than the name of a
peaceable people." Not fighting "when wrongfully
Invaded" will require "great self-denial and Resignation of ourselves to God," something of "that Spirit
in which our Redeemer gave his life for us." Men
of the past, "our predecessors," as well as "many
now living, have learned this blessed lesson." But,
and the plain statement has blasting finality, "many
others, having their Religion chiefly by Education,
and not being enough acquainted with that Cross

which Crucifies to the world, do manifest a Temper distinguishable from that of an Entire trust in God."

With such arguments, though the Assembly was caving in and Franklin was commanding public opinion, though the casualty reports flooded in, and though delegations of indignant Germans waited upon "General Franklin" and paraded a bloody, mutilated corpse through the streets to bring home to Philadelphia the facts of their anguish, Woolman drove a divided body of Quaker elders. "It was a Conference the most weighty that I was ever at," he said. Extraordinarily, since the "sense of the meeting" was divided, the radicals persisted until "Some Friends . . . who appeared easy to pay the tax . . . withdrew. . . ." Finally the "Epistle of Caution," written by Woolman and edited by the remnants of the committee, was issued. It announced that no gloss of compromise, expediency, mixed motives, or accommodation would permit the signers to contribute taxes to "wars and fightings, . . . though suffering be the Consequence of our refusal. . . ."

Without having in the least intended it, following the course of his inward response to the logic of events, John Woolman had emerged as a prophetic radical.

Chapter V

PROFIT AND LOSS

The 13 day, 2 month, 1757 being in good health and abroad with Friends visiting families, I lodged at a Friends house in Burlington, and going to bed about the time usual with me, I awoke in the night and my meditations as I lay were on the goodness and Mercy of the Lord, in a sense whereof my heart was contrite. After this I went to sleep again, and sleeping a short time, I awoke. It was yet dark and no appearance of day nor moonshine, and as I opened my eyes I saw a light in the chamber at the apparent distance of five feet, about nine inches in diameter, of a clear easy brightness, and near the center the most radiant. As I lay still without any surprise looking upon it, words were spoken to my inward ear which filled my whole inward man. They were not the effect of thought, nor any conclusion in relation to the appearance, But as the language of the Holy One Spoken in my mind: the words were *Certain Evidence of Divine Truth,* and were again repeated exactly in the same manner, whereupon the light disappeared.

* * * * * *

The sense I had of the state of the churches, brought a weight of distress upon me. . . . It appeared to me, that through the prevailing of the spirit of this world, the minds of many were brought unto an inward desolation, and instead of the Spirit of Meekness, Gentleness, and Heavenly Wisdom, which are the necessary Companions of the true Sheep of Christ, a Spirit of fierceness, and the love of dominion too generally prevailed.

In the year 1756 Woolman would find it necessary to go out of business, and the Quakers, as such, out of the Assembly, out of control of their province. Controversy ensued among those Quakers who paid the war tax and those who did not, those who, "the Collectors and Constables being Friends," suffered "distress . . . on their goods," and those who exercised the distraints rather than resign their offices. In 1756 the Yearly Meeting declined an invitation by the radicals to investigate their conduct; and a committee which did investigate in 1757 found "publick discussions" of the "diversity of Sentiments" to be "not proper." Radical domination of "the Quaker revival" was the more confirmed.

That radicalism seems to have had aspects of the right, the center, and the left. To the right lay the strenuous Pemberton effort to capture and continue, and continue in, the inherited apparatus of Quaker dominance even though it was out of power. Pembertonism provided a point to which reformed Quaker politicians and relativists could rally. The Yearly Meeting not only discouraged but ultimately discountenanced and forbade politics, and those who were willing to disengage themselves relatively from the world could follow the outlets to power and influence which have been effectively traced in Professor Sydney James's history: private philanthropy; organized charities; humanitarian institutions to do good, expressing Quaker concerns and influencing public opinion.

Those relativists who could not rally to the Pemberton effort found themselves pressed hard by a force of the center wielded by Samuel Fothergill. The son of the intellectually and politically ablest English Friend of his generation, Fothergill had begun in 1754 a mission to the compromised Quakers of the American culture, a mission of purification, a mission of conformity to the conditions and postures of Quakers on the other side of the Atlantic. In England the Friends had become a cultural enclave, an entrenched, encapsulated religiocultural phenomenon within the larger culture. Frozen fast in defensive postures while the life around changed swiftly, English Quakerism had become encysted behind the walls of peculiar dress, speech, and manners, a parochial education, an increasingly rigid and probing discipline which punished nonconformity with expulsion. All this Fothergill preached vigorously. New simplicity, new strictness of distinction from the world, new vigor of institutional discipline at every level, from the family up through the Yearly Meeting, and with minute attention to details, were his watchwords. Those who held back might leave or be disowned.

An interesting fact about the three "wings" of the new Quaker radicalism was that they did not split off and clash (not in this time, at any rate). The Fothergill way was the way of the passive hedgehog—draw in, fortify, build up inner tension to resist outer pressure. And that way of the hedgehog fitted well with the Pemberton way, which was the way of institutional and psychological "empire building." A tight-knit, controllable Society, ever better disciplined, could continue a force, maintain its position, and express its concerns. The Pemberton aggressive and the Fothergill passive hedgehogs could be one.

But hedgehogism would seem clearly unsuited to John Woolman. He was not an epigone but an original, a prophet, a creator with the freedom of a lover and a saint. He was no hedgehog, he was a fox. Woolman needed room and liberty to think and do his work. The paradox of Woolman's situation seems to have been much like that of Francis of Assisi in the church of his time. He could both do and not do his work, realize himself but not wholly, in his circumstances. The dilemma was that there really was nowhere else to go. To have attempted revolution like Benjamin Lay would have been stultifying.

Woolman had to make the best he could of his historical moment. In joining with Churchman, Benezet, and others to promote the revival, the left-wing purity of Quaker radicalism, he inescapably and even gladly (though also with much inner anguish) promoted the encapsulization of the reformed Quaker culture. Creativity warred with prospective fossilization in a set of paradoxes still unresolved. And not the Society or the culture alone but John Woolman also would pay the price. His originality would war, in a context of growing turmoil, with a tendency to mere eccentricity. His problems of judgment would become increasingly acute as his prophetic, intellectual, and expressive achievements grew. There would be profit and loss.

One aspect of the dilemma was illustrated by a discussion Woolman held one August evening while on a circuit through Chester and Philadelphia counties. A Quaker justice of the peace—a relativist and responsibilitist of the old culture's way—came to debate with Woolman, "in calmness and Good Will," the question of not paying taxes. As a JP, the visitor had no doubt suffered under the duty of ordering the confiscation of the property of nonpaying Friends. Trading "in a Brotherly way . . . Some texts of Scripture," the debaters got Woolman's position clearly defined. Then the JP "said he would propose a Medium": those who disagreed with governmental acts should "rather Remonstrate" than refuse their taxes.

The reason offered for this *via media* by the visitor was interesting and inherently appealing to Woolman. Clearly a Christian, the JP offered to argue also—as Woolman was wont to blend the two modes of thought in attacking slavery—from the social-contract ideas of the Enlightenment just then so powerfully in the ascendancy in provincial America that they would soon form the ground for both the Declaration of Independence and the Constitution of the United States. "Civil Government," said the JP, "is an agreement of free men, by which they Oblige themselves to Abide by Certain Laws as a Standard, and to refuse to Obey in that Case is of the like nature as to refuse to do any particular act which we had Covenanted to do."

Woolman's answer doubtless won the debate, but it may really have lost him the point. He replied that it was important "in making Covenants" not "to foreclose ourselves from adhering strictly to true Virtue. . . ." Should he, for instance, "unwarily promise" to obey someone's orders and then be ordered "to assist in doing some great Wickedness," he must suffer the consequences of disobedience rather than obey. It was an efficient debater's answer and altogether right in the abstract. But it was not typical of Woolman in the rigidity of its abstractness and in its distance from the complex human realities of the context of the discussion. Perhaps to the justice, as it would have to Benjamin Franklin, John Adams, or Thomas Jefferson, Woolman's answer sounded more canny than candid. For the Quaker radical there were profits and losses.

I

On the other hand, though he received indispensable help from others, Woolman could be entirely and uniquely himself in the struggle against slavery. On that front there were positive returns, broad, quick, highly satisfactory gains. In 1757 he set out for a two-month-long, 1,150-mile swing through Maryland, Virginia, and North Carolina with a "testimony" in mind. Unlike the dramatic and shocking testimonies of Benjamin Lay, this was a psychological device typical of Woolman. It would be done quietly, in sympathy and even "tenderness," yet it was calculated to get painfully under the skins of those testified against. As a traveling "publick minister" to a lonely and often hard-pressed "people"— and as in his case a minister especially welcome for the freshness and beauty of his "openings"—John Woolman was on several accounts entitled to an eager hospitality. But now he had encountered "a difficulty . . . in [his] mind with respect to saving [his] own money by kindness received, which appeared to [him] to be the gain of Oppression."

Because "conduct is more convincing than language," Woolman, embarrassed, "and in great Abasement, with many tears," won the courage, having been well entertained where slave labor provided the wealth, to prevail upon stricken hosts to

[95]

take the silver pieces he carried, with the explanation that the money was to go "to such of their Negroes as they believed would make the best use of them." Or, if necessary, he "gave them to the Negroes" himself. Although in conventional terms he was delivering a deadly insult, he was able to do it in such a way that "few, if any manifested any resentment at the offer, and most of them, after some little talk, accepted of them." Benjamin Lay would have been thrown out bodily.

Traveling, witnessing, and talking as well as meditating in the saddle, Woolman "often felt language rise from the Centre of [his] mind." Sometimes he spoke, preferring to discuss slavery in meetings for discipline, not worship, the prophetic language of mystical experience. Sometimes, face to face, he spoke the language of persuasive rational discourse. In either case he found winged words. Significantly of Woolman, it is the rational discourse which is recorded in the *Journal.* His argument against slavery, fitted for the mind of the marketplace, was deepening in force and bite.

He pointed out to an accompanying "Colonel of the Militia" how much happier were the lives of people who lived on their own labor than those who lived on slaves. The colonel agreed and blamed "The odds" on the laziness of the slaves—it made the lives of the masters so unhappy. Woolman replied that free men had something to work for, and that he "believed that Liberty was the Natural right of all men equally." This the colonel "did not deny," but said that Negroes were "so wretched in their own Country" that they were better off as slaves here, and the conversation ended.

The next time the latter argument was urged in support of slavery, Woolman was ready for it. If the "real motives" of "fetching [Africans] away for Slaves" were compassionate, he said, then we ought to do all in kindness and sympathy we could to make their lives happy and to lift them up. But if "the white people" simply exploit them, "that burthen will grow heavier and heavier, till times change in a way disagreeable to us." The so-called biblical arguments for slavery he crushed with biblical ease, and the miseries, cruelty, ignorance, and indecencies under which too many slaves were forced to live, he listed exactly and condemned. His logic he could sum up with devastating clarity:

These are a people by whose labour the other inhabitants are in a great measure supported and many of them in the Luxuries of Life. These are a people who have made no agreement to serve us, and have not forfeited their Liberty that we know of. These are souls for whom Christ died and for our conduct toward them, we must answer before that Almighty Being who is no respecter of persons.

As events unfolded, it was fortunate for Woolman that he had become so clearly prepared. After a year of troubles in a countryside increasingly disturbed by the currents of war and in which he had to hold resolutely to his pacifism, he came to the 1758 Yearly Meeting knowing he was in for a crucial political fight over the slavery issue. He would have to use spiritual—and political—weapons. In 1755 the Yearly Meeting had adopted a Minute directing the "overseers" to report "such transgressors" as were "concerned in importing or buying slaves" for disciplinary dealings—and for prospective

disownment. Now certain members of the Philadelphia Monthly Meeting had defiantly purchased
slaves and were seeking to have the prohibition re-
versed and their defiance countenanced.

The historical inference appears to be that the
conservative relativists, the old compromisers, de-
spairing of regaining provincial political power,
chose to stop the sweep of the reformers through the
Quaker culture at the line of the slavery issue. It
was the kind of political situation, one in which
progress toward an ideal good becomes entangled
in irrational and morally cloudy contingencies,
which is calculated to drive a reformer or an idealist
wild with frustration. That Woolman rose above
temptations to anger and flamboyant maneuvering
and that he won his fight on his own terms provides
another measure of the man.

He was helped by his allies, no doubt, and by
certain strategic factors. For one thing, it was at
this same meeting that the decision was taken to
bar all members from political office—and powerful
conservatives were involved. Secondly, moved by
Samuel Fothergill and "inspired by Woolman's
pamphlet and . . . Philadelphia Epistle of 1754," [1]
London Yearly Meeting, the Vatican of Quakerism,
had just issued an epistle condemning trade in
slaves. So Woolman sat in stricken silence through
the other business of the meetings and then, after
others had preceded him in supporting the antislavery position, spoke directly to the prophetic
heart of the matter: the Truth is what counts; humility will bring clear understanding. "The case is
difficult to Some who have [slaves], but if such set
aside all self-interest . . . they will know how to
steer through those difficulties."

---

[1] Drake, p. 60.

Now no one would speak for "Slave Keeping," but there was anxiety lest going too fast should alienate Friends; there was repetition of traditional advice to wait for God to solve the problem. And Woolman was moved to words now famous:

My mind is often led to consider the purity of the Divine Being, and the Justice of his Judgments and herein my Soul is covered with awfullness. I cannot omit to hint of some cases, where people have not been treated with the purity of justice, and the event hath been lamentable. Many Slaves on this continent are oppressed, and their cries have reached the ears of the Most High! Such are the purity and certainty of his judgments, that he cannot be partial toward any. In infinite love and goodness he hath opened our understandings from time to time respecting our duty toward this people, and it is not a time for delay. Should we now be sensible of what he requires of us, and through a respect to the outward interest of some persons, or through a regard to some friendships which do not stand on the immutable foundation, neglect to do our duty in firmness and constancy, still waiting for some extraordinary means to bring about their freedom, it may be that by *Terrible things in Righteousness* God may answer us in this matter.

What Woolman had spoken, without of course knowing it, was a Quaker form of what Professor Perry Miller noted in the literature of the decline of the New England theocracy as a sermon art form, the "Jeremiad." [2] It was a natural form for

[2] *New England Mind*, Vol. 2, *From Colony to Province*, (Cambridge: Harvard University Press, 1953).

the American radical recalling his auditors to the standard of a primitive ideal. In essence it rehearsed the goodness of God in providing for His people in America, pointed to their sins against that goodness, and threatened divine retribution unless there were repentance. The implied historical sense, especially as it applied to the oppression of slaves and Indians, would grow upon Woolman. For the nonce, his expression of it clinched victory in place of the defeat conservatives had planned for him. The Yearly Meeting now adopted a historic Minute expressing "unanimous concern" against "importing, buying, selling, or keeping slaves. . . ." It echoed Woolman's admonitions and, that Friends might be "generally excited" to the practice of the Golden Rule, it appointed John Woolman, John Scarborough, John Sykes, and Daniel Stanton a committee to "visit and treat" with slaveholders.

In the succeeding four years that committee appointment provided Woolman a chance to do one of the things he did best—to deal face to face, with sympathy yet candid witness to "Truth," with erring Friends. He became still more gently direct, learning to be brief in meetings: "In 300 minutes are 5 hours and he that improperly detains three hundred people one minute in a Meeting, besides other Evils that attend it, does an injury like that of Imprisoning one man 5 hours without cause." At this task he was successful both in his own right and in strengthening others to the same work. Eventually the Society would be "clear" of slavekeeping.

Needless to say, this was not done without resentment and pain. A reconciler, as Mrs. Whitney says, "of superb mental health," [3] Woolman still

―――――――
[3] *Op. cit.*, p. 249.

made his enemies, met resistance he could not overcome, and poured out his resources of stamina,
sensitivity, and courage from as deep as he could
reach for them. Though the determined serenity
of the *Journal* (especially in its increasingly "edited"
versions) largely conceals the fact, an irony of
Woolman's relation to the traditions of the Quaker
Journalists is that in his case his "sufferings" were
largely inflicted by Friends—slaveholding Friends.

Some idea of the price he was paying can be
gained from the account of his journey, in the
cause of the slave, to Newport, Rhode Island.
Paradoxically, this thriving seaport was a center of
both Quakerism and the infamous African slave
trade. Traveling far from the contexts of his more
familiar work, Woolman found visiting and "dealing" with Yankee slaveholders "unpleasant." These
sinful Friends were commercially harder than
Southern farmers, and at Newport "the great number of Slaves in these parts, and the Continuance of
a Trade from there to Guinea, made deep impression
on me, and my Cries were often put up to my
Father in Secret, that he would enable me to dis-
charge my duty Faithfully. . . ."

He did his duty faithfully—resourcefully, sensitively, persistently—and the work he did bore
revolutionary fruit in a decade's time. But as he
went to the Newport Yearly Meeting "in Bowedness
of Spirit," he was told "that a large number of
slaves were imported from Africa and then put up
for sale by a member of our Society." Woolman was
literally shaken. Typically, he registered his sense
of what happened by his memory of a sentence
from Habakkuk: "When I heard, my Belly trembled,

my lips quivered, my appetite failed and I grew outwardly weak, and I trembled in myself that I might
rest in the day of trouble." Throughout the trip he
grew spiritually stronger and physically weaker.

Home from the long journey, he worked hard at
neglected affairs, bore the weight of the continuing
war, wrote hard—and in the spring suffered a crisis
which would change his life.

II

Freedom from "cumber" through the sacrifice of
his business won for Woolman freedom to write,
and he wrote a good deal in these crucial years
1756–61. By the middle of the period, in fact, he
had really found all his ideas (as is wont to happen
to creative men before they are forty), and after
that it would be a matter of exploring and developing his insights into his own thought. The document
which makes it clear that Woolman had quite come
into his own by the middle of this period is the
tract on Christian perfectionism he printed in 1758
with the wonderfully typical title, *Considerations on
Pure Wisdom and Human Policy: on Labour; on
Schools; and On the Right Use of the Lord's Outward Gifts.*

Each element in that title represented an essay,
though the four were effectively integrated by
theme and progressive development. And they seem
to have come directly out of Woolman's painful
meditations on the war which had convulsed the
Quaker culture, driven the Friends from the Pennsylvania assembly, embroiled Woolman in the tax
controversy, and led him into the leadership of the
radical wing of the new Quakerism. The war had
also broken into the fabric of life at Mount Holly.

Young Quakers submitted to the military draft, others absconded and hid until the trouble was over; a few had the courage to be openly conscientious objectors and openly face the prospective penalties. Some of these came to Woolman for counsel. He had a soldier quartered upon his household, gave him hospitality, refused payment, and found it necessary to explain his position when "the officer" thanked him.

The results of Woolman's ensuing meditations constituted a wholly innocent and radical—a saintly—counsel to Christian perfection. In tone, strategy, concept, theme, and topic, the four essays are so centrally expressive of Woolman that one might simply quote them and summarize the man and mind. The introduction sounds a note of what seems nowadays a startlingly pioneering insight into the ground and spirit of nonviolent resistance:

My Mind hath often been affected with Sorrow, on account of the prevailing of that Spirit, which leads [out] from an humble waiting on the inward Teaching of Christ, to pursue Ways of Living, attended with unnecessary Labor; and which draws forth the Minds of many People to seek after outward Power, and to strive for Riches, which frequently introduce Oppression, and bring forth Wars, and grievous Calamities.

It is with Reverence that I acknowledge the Mercies of our Heavenly Father, who, in Infinite Love, did visit me in my Youth, and wrought a Belief in me, that through true Obedience a state of inward Purity may be known in this Life; in which we may love Mankind in the same Love with which our Redeemer loveth us, and therein learn Resignation to endure Hardships, for the real Good of others.

From this Woolman develops his logic: for lack of a single-minded "Light" within it, "selfish Desires and an imaginary Superiority, darken the Mind." Thence injustice "frequently proceeds," but the best remedy is "to convince the Judgment." For violence opposed to injustice breeds more violence; and, after "Conflicts productive of very great Calamities," minds remain dark. "But where People walk in that pure Light in which all their 'Works are wrought in God'; and under Oppression persevere in the meek Spirit, and abide firm in the Cause of Truth, without actively complying with oppressive Demands, through these the Lord hath often manifested his Power, in opening the understandings of others, to the promoting Righteousness in the Earth." Woolman concludes his introduction by looking to the time when wars shall cease and dedicates his work to hastening that time.

The essay "On Pure Wisdom and Human Policy" commends "Lowliness of Mind . . . Resignation to the Divine Will, and Contentment in suffering for His Cause. . . ." It fastens on the point that "the self-denying life of an humble contrite Christian" must avoid "those Employments which appear profitable" but really "have an Eye toward the Power of Men and the outward Advantage of Wealth." Penetratingly, it observes that right wisdom is not easy to distinguish from false: "If that, called the Wisdom of this world, had no Resemblance of true Wisdom, the Name of Wisdom, I suppose, had not been given to it." In so doing, Woolman meets the problem of "the Protestant ethic" head on. Wastefulness, laziness, and neglect really are vices, he says, and lead to "Want and Distress." Men ought to shun them. But those who "reach forth for Gain in worldly Wisdom," having it "principally in View to get Riches, and Power, and the Friendship of this World . . . fall into divers temptations and Snares." One of the worst of these is confusion about power: "Great Wealth is frequently attended with Power, which nothing but Divine Love can qualify the Mind to use rightly. . . ." Yet both wealth and the process of getting it, like power, corrupt the mind—and may do the same for children to whom it is given. Pure wisdom is better.

"On Labour" becomes from the start a personal and strikingly original "Consideration." Its theme, taken from "Experience," is that "Right Exercise affords an innocent Pleasure in the Time of it, and prepares us to enjoy the Sweetness of Rest; but from the Extremes each Way, arise Inconveniences." Right labor makes us healthy, happy, and harmonious with God's design. But selfish labor, too long, too hard, dulls the mind, destroys physical harmony, and spoils "the Sweetness of Rest." It leads to heat, and hurry, and often to intemperate drink; and "the Mind . . . doth not retain that calmness and Serenity which we should endeavour to live in." Not only the self-employed but the landlords should be careful not to drive tenants to overwork. And the slaveholder especially must see that he is not so defiled. The essay ends with a plea for the aged and worn-out slave, particularly the one who has been left to a callous heir; for if "Youth are often ignorant of the Language of old age, how hard is the Case of ancient Negroes. . . ."

In John Woolman's hands, "On Schools" becomes, once more, a surprisingly "progressive" sort of essay. "It is a lovely Sight to behold innocent children," said this strange preromantic. "That Divine Light which enlightens all Men, I believe, does often shine in the Minds of Children very early. . . ." Therefore, he argues, they should not be urged to learning for "the Spirit of Pride and the Love of Praise" (he never so much as mentions the fear of the whip, which would still for generations be a principal motivation of the little American scholar). On the contrary, children need tutors "acquainted with Sanctification of Spirit"—good Quakers, in short—who will have few enough pupils to be able to so "weightily attend to the Spirit and Conduct of each Individual, as to be enabled to administer rightly to all in due Season"; for "to help them against that which would mar the Beauty of their Minds, is a Debt we owe them. . . ." When this was published, Mary Woolman was about eight years old. At "several times," mostly in the next decade (the dates are obscure), Woolman would himself keep school in Mount Holly; and he wrote and published a primer.

Given the foregoing, "On the Right Use of the Lord's Outward Gifts" was reasonably predictable. It caps the climax of the work with a stress on the economic which was new, if not in substance, in emphasis in Quaker writing. It attacked the conservative-relativist "grandees" almost by name and extended the sensibility of the radicals by a degree and more of modernity. Woolman's accent fell on the psychospiritual source in "Pride or Self-love" and "the Desire after worldly Greatness" of conspicuous consumption. The corresponding stress fell on a simplicity which freed the mind to pursue "the peaceable Government of Christ."

Much more interesting, because it was less predictable and obviously calculated to explode like a mine in Philadelphia, was an essay suppressed by the desires of "the overseers of the press" that it be "deferred" from the 1758 publication. Called "Serious Considerations on Trade," it was never published until included in the Gummere edition of 1922, and the reason why becomes clear as one reads through its twelve placidly logical paragraphs: Woolman was promoting consideration of the abolition of all ordinary intercontinental or overseas trade.

He begins by establishing the unity of the peoples of the earth and the necessity of preaching the Gospel everywhere: so the seas must "sometimes" be crossed. And in the settling of "a Wilderness" there must be trade and supply—but what after the settlements are actually self-supporting? Then "Customs contrary to pure wisdom" need re-examination. Are the human costs of trade—the ships, goods, and sailors lost at sea, the people wastefully employed, oppressed, punished, and distracted in affairs not of "real service"—worth it? Think of the costs of imperial trade wars "between different branches of the great family." "O how precious is the Spirit of peace!" in ". . . that true simplicity where no wandering desires lead on to strife, where no treasures possessed in a selfish Spirit tend to beget ill will in other selfish men. And where true love so seasons their proceedings, that the pure witness is reached in such who are well acquainted with them."

Here was a blow too radical even for the Pembertons. The "overseers" said tactfully that they wished it "deferred," and Woolman accepted their judgment in the spirit in which he wrote. He "felt easy" and postponed publication, so far as he knew, forever. The Quaker radicals had on their hands not only a spiritual but an economic prophet of the most radical possible type—he proposed quietly to substitute Christian love for every type of economic motivation or explanation. And precisely because he wrote genuinely from that point of view, he was not frustrated at this temporary silencing. The idea would recur naturally, and he had much yet to write.

III

Probably more or less simultaneously, Woolman continued to work up the second part of *Considerations on the Keeping of Negroes*. He finished it after his return from Newport; and when it was published in 1762 it was a considerably more aggressive document than its predecessor. Where Part I had begun in an atmosphere of sweet reasonableness, the Preface to this strikes out in the bold paradoxes of what are virtually metaphysical conceits and certainly biting irony. Only God can really judge man's actions, says Woolman: "I believe that one Supreme Being made and supports the World; nor can I worship any other Deity without being an Idolator and guilty of Wickedness."

But, though pagans of many nations have worshiped "a Plurality of Deities," they were not necessarily wicked. Many professing Christians are really idolators of "the Honors, Profits and Friendships of the World"; and "the Gentile," even with his mistaken opinions, may actually be "established in the true Principle of Virtue, and . . . fear God and work righteousness." Woolman cannot accept "the Bishop of Rome," but to say of the Pope's followers "that none of them are upright in Heart, would be contrary to [his] Sentiments." Regardless, in short, of whatever "speculative and great Errors" any heretic may believe, men who "love God sincerely, and prefer the real Good of Mankind universally to their own private Interest" may be saved. In fact, at the climax of the Preface, though "we have no right to keep men as Servants for Term of Life, but that of superior Power" and to "Design by their Labor to profit ourselves and our Families . . . is wrong," nevertheless, not all keepers of slaves "have therefore been chargeable with Guilt"—not "if their Motives thereto were free from Selfishness"!

Thematically basic to the whole of Part II is a recurrent trope of gathering historical darkness: "Where Unrighteousness is justified from one Age to another, it is like dark Matter gathering into clouds over us. We may know that this Gloom will remain till the Cause be removed by a Reformation, or change of Times. . . ." But Woolman is too honest to indulge in the illusions of the romantic liberal that the way of regeneration will be easy. The reformer must be willing to *endure Hardness on that account.*" This leads him to consider the biblical prophets, and they in turn lead him to an extended refutation on biblical grounds of the biblical argument for slavery and racial discrimination—which has been so often laid to rest and disinterred in moldy stubbornness by the ignorant and unscrupulous. And from this he emerges with the principle of the Preface: At the end of the ends, "if we keep them from no other Motive than a real Sense of

Duty, and true charity governs us in all our Proceedings toward them, we are so far safe"—but who dare make such claims?

Furthermore, Woolman urges, while a real missionary motivation to "undergo hardships for their Sakes" might be admirable, the whole actual course of slave taking, dealing, and keeping is the opposite. Not only is it constantly productive of real evils, but it exposes the human psyche to every worst perversion. His moral insights at this key point seem strikingly modern:

Forced Subjection on innocent Persons of full Age, is inconsistent with right Reason; on one side, the human Mind is not naturally fortified with that Firmness in Wisdom and Goodness necessary to an independent Ruler; on the other Side, to be subject to the uncontrollable Will of a Man, liable to err, is most painful and afflicting to a conscientious Creature.

It is our Happiness faithfully to serve the Divine Being, who made us. His Perfection makes our Service reasonable; but so long as Men are biassed by Narrow Self-love, so long an absolute Power over other Men is unfit for them.

Men, taking on them the Government of others, may intend to govern reasonably, and to make their Subjects more happy than they would be otherwise; but, as absolute Command belongs only to him who is perfect, where frail Men, in their own Wills, assume such Command, it hath a direct Tendency to vitiate their Minds, and make them more unfit for Government.

Slavery humiliates the slave, degrades him to a seeming subhuman, and dangerously exalts the master. It betrays masters into the infliction of cruelties (even one Quaker woman in New England had lashed a slave to death) and into violation of Woolman's insights into right labor. Instead of whipping up conventional horror over the description of slave families and forced immoralities, Woolman attacked with a moment of conjugal hymnody and the *argumentum ad hominem*. In "the human Species," weakness and vulnerability in child-bearing and the helplessness of the young ". . . clearly show that *Perfect Goodness* designs a tender Care and Regard should be exercised toward them; and that no imperfect Power should prevent the cordial Effects of that Sympathy, which is in the Minds of well-met Pairs to each other, and toward their Offspring." But the success of slave marriages often "depends on the Will of Men, liable to human Passions and a bias in Judgment. . . . These Things being considered closely as happening to a near Friend, will appear to be hard and painful."

In fact, says Woolman, modulating at midpoint into the dominating thematic trope of the essay, if we should think of slaves as we do of ordinary people—white people—slavery would seem impossible. He cites travelers to show that Negroes at home in Africa were intelligent and happy; Senegal was a primitive paradise. The trouble is that our minds are entangled in the custom of twisted, false ideas. We are like a traveler lost in gloom and fog and disoriented, insisting that east is west and so entangled in "false Notions" that even after the appearance of the sun he finds it hard to accept the truth. "Selfishness being indulged, clouds the

Understanding." This and custom darken our reason and let us suppose that color makes Negroes
liable to slavery, although "their Understandings
and Morals are equal to the Generality of Men of
[our] own Color," and although "the Color of a
Man avails nothing in Matters of Right and Equity."

The remainder of the essay seeks to dispel the
clouds of "Self-love" and let the reader see the
realities of the situation of the slave, the need to
identify with the slave as a victimized person, and
the need to abandon aspiration "after Imaginary
Grandeur" and to treat the Negro with sympathy
and "true charity." Eyewitness accounts of the bar-
barities and atrocities of the African slave trade
are quoted. The complicity of the civilized Christian slavekeeper with those horrors is established,
the contradictions with every motive of Christianity,
justice, and humanitarianism are emphasized, and
the results of the most ordinary empathy with the
slave are suggested. Finally Woolman turns with
something like scorn to the Quaker argument that,
although enslavement was wicked and slave buying
wrong, slavekeeping is unavoidable both for the
good of the slave (who would otherwise be cast out
to starve and steal) and of the society (which
could not afford the irruption upon it of a freed
black proletariat). The reply is crisp: Negro slaves
for seventy years past have built up colonial wealth
—they have an equity in it and a right to a fair share;
some might become indigent or criminal, but there
is social machinery to cope with that. The summary
conclusion, to "answer all our Objections," is "that
Liberty is the Right of innocent Men; that the
Mighty God is a Refuge for the Oppressed; that
they being set free, are still liable to the Penalties
of our Laws. . . ."

At the climax, recurring finally to his leitmotiv, Woolman turned it, gently but piercingly, into a Quaker jeremiad:

From one age to another, the Gloom grows thicker and darker . . . where, through the Agreement of a Multitude, some channels of Justice are stopped, . . . there is great Danger of contracting an Alliance with that Spirit which stands in Opposition to the God of Love, and spreads Discord, Trouble, and Vexation. . . .

Negroes are our Fellow Creatures, and their present Condition amongst us requires our serious Consideration. We know not the Time when those Scales in which Mountains are weighed, may turn. The Parent of Mankind is gracious; His Care is over His smallest Creatures; and a Multitude of men Escape not His Notice. And though many of them are trodden down, and despised, yet he remembers them: He seeth their Affliction, and looketh upon the spreading, increasing Exaltation of the Oppressor. He turns the Channels of Power, humbles the most haughty People, and gives Deliverance to the Oppressed at such periods as are consistent with His infinite Justice and Goodness. And wherever Gain is preferred to Equity, and wrong Things publickly encouraged, to that Degree that Wickedness takes Root, and spreads wide amongst the Inhabitants of a Country, there is real Cause for Sorrow to all such whose Love to Mankind stands on a true Principle, and who wisely consider the End and Event of Things.

Chapter VI

THE ECCENTRIC ORBIT:
THE LARGER MISSION

In a time of Sickness with the pleurisy a little upward of two years and a half ago, I was brought so Near the gates of death, that I forgot my name. Being then desirous to know who I was, I saw a mass of matter of a dull gloomy colour, between the South and the East, and was informed that this mass was human beings, in as great misery as they could be, and live, and that I was mixed in with them, and henceforth I might not consider myself as a distinct or Separate being. In this state I remained several hours. I then heard a soft Melodious voice, more pure and harmonious than any voice I had heard with my ears before, and I believed it was the voice of an angel who spake to the other angels. The words were *John Woolman is dead.* I soon remembered that I once was John Woolman, and being assured that I was alive in the body, I greatly wondered what that heavenly voice could mean.

I believed beyond doubting that it was the voice of an holy Angel, but as yet it was a mystery to me.

I was then carried in Spirit to the mines, where poor Oppressed people were digging rich treasures for those called Christians, and heard them blaspheme the name of Christ, at which I was grieved for his Name to me was precious.

Then I was informed that these heathen were told that those who oppressed them were the followers of Christ; and they said amongst themselves, If Christ directed them to use us in this Sort then Christ is a cruel tyrant.

All this time the Song of the Angel remained a Mystery, and in the morning my dear wife and some others coming to my bedside I asked them if they knew who I was, and they telling me I was John Woolman, thought I was only light-headed, for I told them not what the Angel said, nor was I disposed to talk much to any one; but was very desirous to get so deep that I might understand this Mystery.

My tongue was often so dry that I could not speak till I had moved it about and gathered some moisture, and as I lay still for a time, at length I felt divine power prepare my mouth that I could speak, and then I said, "I am crucified with Christ, nevertheless I live; yet not I, but Christ liveth in me, and the life I now live in the flesh is by faith in the Son of God who loved me and gave himself for me."

Then the Mystery was opened and I perceived there was Joy in heaven over a Sinner who had repented, and that that language, *John Woolman is dead,* meant no more than the death of my own will.

The final dozen years of John Woolman's life have not been clearly elucidated by his biographers. And it is difficult to perceive just what was the

significant pattern of those years. Perhaps the truth
is that conflicting impulses swirled about and within Woolman, pulling him in opposite directions and
distorting the patterns of fulfillment toward which
his life tried to grow. After the Newport venture,
quite naturally and no doubt voluntarily, he disappeared from the center of Quaker revival politics.
His works of visitation continued, and the mission
to abolish slavery from the Society of Friends was
set on the road to final success. But beneath the
surface of his gentle ministry and the wholesome
round of Mount Holly life, Woolman's inner life
deepened and darkened toward new prophetic vi-
olences—the ghost of Benjamin Lay beckoned in the
background, and "concerns" for large missions, perhaps quixotic, kept stirring in Woolman's conscience. He also had the time, the creative impulse,
and at last, apparently, the habit of composition to
permit him to do what was, for him, a great deal of
writing.

I

It will not do to gloss over or sentimentalize the
psychic clashes and their consequences in Woolman's intellectual as well as personal experiences
after his fortieth year. The actual record is clear.
Apparently, during the strain of his long-extended
Newport mission through the heats of summer,
Woolman's highly sensitized mind had returned to
earlier meditations on simplicity, purity, plainness,
cleanliness, abstention from use of slave products,
and natural health. As the *Journal* says, ". . . thinking often on these things, the use of hats and garments dyed with a dye hurtful to them, and wearing
more clothes in summer than are useful grew more

uneasy to me, believing them to be customs which have not their foundation in pure wisdom." Quaker conformity bound him, however, and, "The apprehension of being Singular from my Beloved Friends was a strait upon me, and thus I remained in the Use of Some things contrary to my Judgment."

On the last day of May, 1761, he fell "ill of a fever" [1] and suffered it "in great distress of Body" for a week—which set him searching for the cause of his "Chastisement" and "the design of [his] Correction." Having achieved complete "Resignation," he felt "an inward healing in [his] Nature" and began to get well. Thereafter he became settled in his mind "in relation to hurtful dyes."

As John Woolman, not Benjamin Lay, he did nothing sudden or dramatic about his new commitment. He decided simply to wear out his old, dyed things and replace them as necessary with undyed raiment. It should not be presumed that Woolman intended thereafter to go about in dazzling white like the later Mark Twain. His cloth would be the natural and beautifully plain tone of homespun fabric. Nor does the tradition seem justified that his hat was to be white.[2] As he says twice in one paragraph of the *Journal*, his worst trial in regard to "Affecting Singularity" concerned "a hat the natural colour of the fur"—the more especially because such hats were at the moment the fashion amongst those

---

[1] Mrs. Gummere guesses that this "fever" was a return of boyhood "fever and ague" for a resident of the long-famous "Skeeter State" (*Journal*, p. 246). Mrs. Whitney (p. 276) guesses that it was a bad case of flu. A psychosomatically minded guesser might see wider implications—but nobody really knows.

[2] Presumably bowing to the tradition, Mrs. Whitney (p. 277) sees Woolman in "white beaver" after quoting him on "the natural color of the fur"—but beaver is never naturally (except perhaps in very rare albinism) white; and, as Mrs. Gummere notes, the tradition of the white hat seems to rest on an addendum to the *Journal* manuscript "in a later hand" (n. 1, p. 247).

worldlings "who were fond of following the change-
able modes of dress. . . ." Woolman came sharply
into conflict with the Fothergill-Pemberton drive
toward disciplined uniformity. He became an ec-
centric and, worse, felt inwardly checked from ex-
plaining more when dealt with, than, "that I believed my wearing it was not in my own will." Some
Friends "carried Shy" of him; his ministry was "shut
up" for a while; "many Friends" became "uneasy"
with him; and he had reason to feel purged of the
dangers of "superficial friendship" until "the Lord
in his own time would open the hearts of Friends
toward [him]." Here was "singularity" indeed.

The whole record, moreover, suggests that Woolman's change of clothing bespoke a change of inner
weather and that his sartorial singularity symbolized
a certain withdrawal from even the neo-Quaker
culture being forged by the radical Friends for
whom he was becoming, rather elusively, too radical. Gently, tenderly, without a touch of Benjamin
Lay's militancy, cooperating as much as he could
wherever he could, Woolman was stepping aside.
In a modern context, one would be tempted to say
that he was behaving not only like a saint but like
an artist. And perhaps he was.

It was at this point, in fact, that Woolman came
hard up against the American saint's dilemma. In a
context in which it has traditionally been difficult
if not impossible to damn the culture completely
or finally (since one always has the complicit guilt
of having helped to make it and the opportunity to
help remake it), the American saint—and artist—
stands caught between the kingdom of heaven and
the culture, between purity and compromise, between the ideal and the pragmatic, the transcendent and the human. If he does not compromise,

he prices himself out of the market of men's hearts; if he does, the purity and force of his work and witness are lost. In an Emersonian ideal beyond idealism, there might be the chance to have one's cake and eat it—to move transcendently above humanity yet stoop to create new glories for it (and in his writings Woolman did that). More ordinarily, the prices must be paid of loneliness, eccentricity, even error, for the hope that something said or done will strike an answering chord in the hearts of the multitude and so contribute something to the salvation of the culture even though the contributor be lost (at least culturally) for it.

Thus, Woolman testified with increasing alienation from his times. In his queer garments, he gave up the use of sugar, molasses, rum, and silver— because they were the products largely of slave labor, were luxurious superfluities corrupting to the rich and grinding upon the poor. He knew how he struck again at Philadelphia's trade; and he witnessed with tears, but he witnessed. Because Quaker meetings, including his own, would not admit Negroes to membership, he took the daring step of convening a meeting in his own home for the purpose of regularly marrying a slave and his freed-slave fiancée. As he took his journeys into the South for the slave in the 1760's, despite growing physical debility he traveled on foot: as a testimony of simplicity; as an act of empathetic identification with the sufferings of slaves; as an added means of leverage against the consciences of Quaker slave-keepers.

He went off to the wilderness to visit with the Indians. He sat and reasoned with Mount Holly folk who had gathered at a neighboring tavern to

see a juggler perform—arguing that it was un-
Christian—and no doubt spoiled the evening. He
became, in the town recollection, "peculiar and
felt his mind often straitened in small things." He
developed a fixation about coming into Meeting on
the dot, and, to do so, often arrived early and sat
outside on the horse block to wait.[3] In short, John
Woolman was developing a vein of genuine and
rather tormented eccentricity. He was also, however,
developing his peculiar expressive genius toward
its literary peak.

II

A Plea for the Poor, possibly written as early as
1763–64 but not published in Woolman's lifetime,
varies the themes of *Considerations on Pure Wisdom*. Perhaps the most carefully structured of
Woolman's works, it articulates all his ideas in a
style more blunt in the rather dry directness of its
tactics than the earlier sets of gracefully hinting
Considerations, but less eloquently prophetic and
with considerably less of Woolman's winning sweetness of personality. Aside from the plain-speaking
boldness (does one catch a certain note of im-
patience if not irritation new to Woolman?), the
principal features new in *A Plea for the Poor* are
the increased concern for animals included in Woolman's theory of right labor; the lessons on how to
pass through the eye of the needle—how to be a
good rich man—with the attendant incisive observations on how much more effective are the poor in
doing good than the rich; the inclusion of the Indian as an object of concern; and a clear-cut state-

---

[3] Cox, "Sketches . . . ," p. 24.

ment of Woolman's preference (had it been affected by physiocratic theories currently fashionable?) for an agrarian way of life from which, like Thomas Jefferson, Woolman was anxious to exclude notions of gentry-building primogeniture.

The argument of *A Plea for the Poor* flows smoothly from topic to topic in Woolman's blend of logic and association. "Wealth desired for its own sake Obstructs the increase of Virtue," he begins typically, and closes his introduction, having contrasted vice and virtue in material life, with his central theme: "While industrious frugal people are borne down with poverty, and oppressed with too much labour in useful things, the way to apply money, without promoting pride and Vanity, remains open to such as truly Sympathize with them in their various Difficulties." Only God owns the universe, he continues, and we must obey His laws of mercy, justice, and harmony as His tenants. And this raises the question of how to be rich and good: it "requires close attention to *Divine love.*" Insofar as that "Love influences Our minds," so far "we become interested in His workmanship, and feel a desire to take hold of every opportunity to lessen the distresses of the Afflicted, and increase the Happiness of the Creation . . . to turn all the treasures we possess into the channel of Universal Love, becomes the business of our lives." Thus Woolman is led to something like a hymn to the beauties of the good use of wealth. By the rich man's care and humility:

Poor men eased of their burthens, and released from too close an application to business, are at Liberty to hire others to their assistance, to provide well for their Animals, and find time to perform those duties amongst their Acquaintance, which belong to a well guided Social life.

When these reflect on the opportunity those had to oppress them, and consider the goodness of their conduct, they behold it Lovely, and consistent with brotherhood. And as the man whose mind is conformed to Universal Love, hath his Trust Settled in God, and hath a firm Foundation to Stand on in any changes or Revolutions that happen among men; so also, the goodness of his conduct tends to spread a kindly, benevolent disposition in the world.

But in saying this, John Woolman only introduces reflections on the rich man's transcendent need for scrupulous sensitivity and empathy, the demand on him especially for the sacrificial spirit of Christ. Thence, Woolman could move to an observation which would not come to the forefront of American social consciousness until Howells would hammer it into the conscience of the Gilded Age: it is the poor who, sharing deprivation, know how to be charitable (and for Howells, whatever the later effect upon him of Tolstoi, Woolman had been a household name from childhood).[4] To illustrate what the rich man's eyes must be opened to see, Woolman restates his theory of right labor and then hits hard again at a great temptation of Quakers—laying up estates for children. To establish the theological base for his arguments he turns to the

---

[4] See William Cooper Howells, *Recollections of Life in Ohio From 1813 to 1840* (Cincinnati: The Robert Clarke Co., 1895), p. 69; and W. D. Howells, review of Whittier's edition of Woolman's *Journal, Atlantic Monthly*, XXVIII (August, 1871), pp. 251-2.

theology of wealth (true riches lie in God only) and to an attack on the tyranny inherent in idolatry of "the selfish spirit."

It is that selfishness which brings on war, he continues, and a true stewardship, especially of land, would prevent evil. This, Woolman suggests, is the key to the Indian problem. It is also the key to the problems of growing cultural complexity, social differentiation, and social justice. *A Plea for the Poor* was published in 1793 as *A Word of Remembrance and Caution to the Rich.* But when he wrote it, Woolman seems to have been in tune with much of the current economic theory of his age. His religious radicalism tinged it throughout. Where contemporary economic thought emphasized the labor theory of value, Woolman emphasized the debt of riches to the poor. He adumbrated the idea which would be thoroughly radical when Thomas Paine proposed it in *Agrarian Justice* (1797),[5] that every man has an inalienable birthright to his share of the land God has given the whole family in common. Echoes of such thought would stir not only Americans but minds around the world when Henry George set them ringing in *Progress and Poverty* a century after Woolman.

A Plea for the Poor ends with recapitulations of Woolman's views on schools, on relations of masters and servants, and with a compact plea for those poorest of all the poor, the Negroes. Anticipating

---

[5] For the physiocratic influence see Vernon L. Parrington, "The Colonial Mind," *Main Currents in American Thought,* (New York: Harcourt, Brace & Co., 1927), pp. 171–3, *et passim;* Joseph Dorfman, *The Economic Mind in American Civilization, 1606–1865,* I, (New York: Viking Press, 1946), pp. 191–2. Dorfman's compact survey of Woolman's ideas is, unfortunately, not comparative. For Paine, see Harry Hayden Clark, "Introduction," *Thomas Paine,* (New York: American Book Company, 1944), pp. lxxviii–lxxxi.

the pathos of Miss Watson's lucky, hairy-chested
Jim, rich because he owned himself and had a
large market value, Woolman resorts openly to
bookkeeping procedures in figuring the indemnities
with interest owed to Negroes even after liberation.
His final plea for the poor is unpretentiously devastating: "Now when our minds are thoroughly di-
vested of all prejudice in relation to the difference
of colour . . . I believe it will appear that a heavy
account lies against us as a Civil Society for oppressions committed against people who did not
injure us; and that if the particular case of many
individuals were fairly stated, it would appear that
there was considerable due to them."

While *A Plea for the Poor,* perhaps out of tenderness for the uneasiness of his fellow "overseers," lay
unpublished in the pages of his folio, Woolman
wrote, and at the end of the decade published, *Considerations on the True Harmony of Mankind, and
How It Is To Be Maintained.* This set of "Considerations" is at once the most learnedly allusive, the
most biblical, and the most theological of Woolman's writings. The Quaker persona of eighteenth-
century Enlightenment, reasoning independently
from hints of first principles sweetly apprehended
within, was gone. Woolman's rather scholarly stance
was unusual in the main line of Quaker tradition.
And yet, it kept in key with the best of the indig-
enous Quaker culture. Perhaps Woolman's strategy
was to find new ways to appeal to those (both within and without the ranks of the radical party) whose
hearts he felt had been closed to his word. Thus
the voice which speaks in the *True Harmony* is
that of a serious, learned mind, so agonized in its
concern for charity as to feel the need of supreme

authority to support its solemn and ultimately rather minatory message.

The Introduction consists of a single paragraph in which the theme of the suppressed "Serious Considerations on Trade" is shadowed forth. Chapter I, "On Serving the Lord in Our Outward Employments," is new only in the number of its appeals to scriptural and historical authority and in its "brotherly sympathy" for "the condition of many who live in cities." But the next, "On the Example of Christ," presents us, unexpectedly and uniquely, with John Woolman's Christology:

> Jesus Christ had no reserve in promoting the happiness of others; he was not deficient in looking for the helpless . . . ; of whose compassion towards us I may now speak a little.
>
> He who was perfectly happy in himself, moved with infinite love, took not upon himself the nature of angels, but our imperfect natures: and being the SON of HIM who is greater than earthly princes, yet became a companion to poor, sincere-hearted men.

Woolman's is the incarnate, human Christ, rejected, slandered, humilated, tortured, "smitten of God and afflicted." Woolman's doctrine of the atonement is in keeping with all his thought: Christ triumphs over the sin of the world by the reign of his spirit in the hearts of believers, a state "where every motion from a selfish spirit yieldeth to pure love." And the conclusion follows firmly: "Now this mind being in us, which was in Christ Jesus, it removes from our hearts the desire of Superiority, worldly honours, or greatness."

Against this background he can turn in "On Merchandising" to consider his own experience without the slightest personal reference but in the context of the most densely biblical reference Woolman ever wove. Following Christ, "the mind becomes chaste."

In being crucified to the world, broken off from that friendship which is enmity with God, and dead to the Customs and fashions which have not their foundation in the Truth, the way is prepared to lowliness in outward living . . . and where the friends of Christ are so situated that merchandise appears to be their duty . . . they are taught, not only to keep to a moderate advance and uprightness in their dealings; but to consider the tendency of their proceeding; to do nothing which they know would operate against the cause of Universal Righteousness. . . .

From this transcendent point of view Woolman can then glance briefly in closing at "On Divine Admonitions" and hint a jeremiad. He has not said, "Consider whether you should not give up trade." But it now became an open question whether even Israel Pemberton would not stand self-condemned if he honestly examined his relation to the true harmony of mankind.

III

In such contexts Woolman was devoting himself to the intensive period of composition which essentially completed his masterpiece, the *Journal*. Perhaps the one fact most essential to an understanding of that classic is that it was not a diary; it was not "kept" but composed. In this fact it is unlike the diaries of Samuel Sewall, Sarah Kemble Knight, or any of the hosts of survivors of the Puritan habit of daily casting up personal accounts with Providence. It is of a wholly different order from those other treasures of American cultural history, the diaries of Colonel William Byrd of Westover, the indispensable *Journals* of Emerson and Thoreau, or those seedbeds of the "germs" of Hawthorne's genius, his *Notebooks*.

These analogies to Woolman's *Journal* intimate that he stands close to the fountainhead of an American genre. But actually he was composing immediately in a rich and vital tradition of Quaker literature. The early Friends had written furiously, publishing, often by necessary stealth, something on the order of 2,600 pieces by some four hundred and forty different authors before 1709.[6] As Luella M. Wright, still the principal authority, says, between 1650 and 1725 more than forty Quaker "memoirs with homogeneous qualities" were published. The facts that from 1689 to 1725 twenty-six "journals" appeared and between 1726 and 1758 (the heart of Woolman's growing up) fourteen more were produced, show Woolman composing close to the center of a thriving tradition. And as we have seen, there is strong evidence to suggest that not only Woolman's work but his very life was modeled on the common denominators of the Quaker journals.

Quaker-like, a man of the word, Woolman was a keeper and saver of records. It seems the more significant, therefore, that no diaries appear among his

---

[6] Brinton, *Friends for 300 Years*, p. 179.

papers, even though diaries were traditionally acceptable part-sources for journals. The positive evidence for his composition of the *Journal* is the state of the three successive manuscripts. Whether there were once notes from which Woolman worked or whether these manuscripts (or some of them) were fair copies of destroyed originals can probably never be determined. But what those manuscripts reveal plainly, and on their face, to any eye accustomed to deal with literary sources is that, first as a participant in the living traditions of his sect and culture, and secondly as, in his own peculiar way, a literary artist, John Woolman composed his masterpiece.[7]

Woolman's *Journal* became not only the acme of its tradition's achievement but a literary classic in its own right for three main reasons. It expresses and communicates the essential best, the ethos, atmosphere, values, and living inwardness of a singular and interesting culture. As a work of art it presents a personality of extraordinary human sweetness and spiritual beauty. "I hear it was charged against me that I sought to destroy institutions," said Walt Whitman in famous lines, "But really I am neither for nor against institutions." In precisely this sense the Woolman of the *Journal* is uncanonized, noninstitutional and self-made, and thus, an Ameri-

---

[7] This is not a proper place in which to discuss the complex editorial problems regarding Woolman's text. Suffice it to say that those problems became, during the 150 years after Woolman's death, as knotted as those of any other American author—which is saying a great deal. The valiant but unprofessional efforts of Mrs. Gummere disentangled many problems. Mrs. Whitney's essay at the production of a "clear text" (*The Journal of John Woolman*, Chicago: H. Regnery Co., 1950) has been very useful rather than "definitive." It seems to me that there is no doubt that the writings of John Woolman must be kept on the registry of needed tasks of the Center for Editions of American Authors until somebody produces a definitive edition by modern and professional bibliographical means.

can saint. Finally, uniquely and therefore elusively, Woolman's *Journal* is a triumph of style.

Before, let us say, 1750 and during the first thirty years of Woolman's life, the Quaker culture of his region constituted an idyllic moment in history. For all the flaws which would open it to historical destruction (and call John Woolman forth as a reformer), that culture clearly was largely ideal—and who shall say that the historical forces around it would not have broken it up had it been flawless? The triumphs of that culture lay in two realms. It achieved a style of life—free, quiet, wholesome, productive, disciplined, and honest—in which the human spirit could feel organically at home. Certain deep, essential yearnings of man's soul were met and satisfied by such a culture. Further, as the persistent Voltairean idealization of the Quaker (based on some knowledge of that culture) reveals, it presented to a world sick of religious wars, of aristocratic pomposity, vice, and cruelty, and of irrational vanities, the face of genuine alternatives.[8]

In trying to grasp the force of the *Journal* as a work of art, it is perhaps most helpful to begin by trying to see what kind of art it is. One's first impulse, of course, is to reject the notion of its artistry. How could Woolman be an artist? Woolman, who rejected decoration and the consciously aesthetic, even in mere furniture or in the carving of a ship's cabin, as spiritually poisonous "superfluity." Yet nothing can be clearer than the fact that Woolman's aesthetic responses were keen. He reacted profoundly to nature and to the faces and voices of spiritually sympathetic people, and overwhelmingly to the word, to the literature of spiritual revelation.

---

[8] See esp. Edith Philips, *The Good Quaker in French Legend* (Philadelphia: University of Pennsylvania Press, 1932).

Living at the heart of his culture, Woolman, the artist, was forced to use the expressive tools—distressingly few in number—available to him. The tradition of the journals was far and away the aesthetically best expressive mode available. Most fortunately, it was not only traditionally proper but also rich in prophetic prestige. John Woolman needed to feel no conflict when he undertook to express himself in that form.

The religious and cultural conventions regularized in the tradition of the Quaker journal had turned it into a form, a mode of expression, that would have been suspected by no practitioner, including Woolman. But careful study of the major examples is sure to show that they achieve much of their obvious power to stimulate and to order the imaginative experience of the reader because they really are a kind of fiction. This genre, says Northrop Frye in some of the most sensible brief comments available, is that "very important form of prose fiction the confession form." Its examples are "inspired by a creative, and therefore fictional, impulse to select only those events and experiences in the writer's life that go to build up an integrated pattern . . . something larger than himself, or simply the coherence of his character and attitudes." [9]

Obviously the essence of Woolman's *Journal* is the multiple integration of his personal coherences with the drama of his dealings with God in society and God Within. But another way to see what Woolman was about is to notice that the possibility of his work depended upon an act of creation in imagining himself. As contemporary depth psychology suggests, our concepts of our selves are multiple, often

[9] *Anatomy of Criticism* (Princeton: Princeton University Press, 1957), pp. 307–8.

situationally determined, unstable, often vaguely unrecognized or half-glimpsed, and thus hard for the rational and expressive mind to fix. Therefore the selective, determined act of a gifted imagination is required to visualize or perhaps to create the self who shall be the subject and protagonist of a confession.

There is currently a school of what might be called post-Tocquevillean cultural critics who hold that this act—of creating the self within a culture which is itself in process of becoming—is the essential, distinguishing task (always somehow a failure) of the American artist.[10] Whether this theory is, on the whole, strictly true or only a suggestive intellectual device, it illuminates Woolman's *Journal* generically. The *Journal* belongs to a major group of American classics, often thought unclassifiable, but clearly "confession forms" in Frye's sense, and of the most basic significance in Pearce's sense. To it belong Edwards' *Personal Narrative*, Franklin's *Autobiography*, *Walden*, Whitman's *Democratic Vistas*, *The Education of Henry Adams*, and a host of less recognized works.

The meaning and importance of the frequency as well as the high aesthetic power of this form in American literature and culture need more careful study than they have attracted. What, for example, are the relationships to the confession genre of *Moby Dick* and *The Adventures of Huckleberry Finn?* Surely it is significant that major examples appear with the flowering (and with the passing) of provincial American culture. Perhaps the pitifully groping despair of Twain's late works shows what hap-

---

[10] Its leading spokesman is perhaps Roy Harvey Pearce, of whose major work, *The Continuity of American Poetry* (Princeton: Princeton University Press, 1961), this is an informing idea.

pens when the "confession form" ceases to be available. Not only does Woolman's *Journal* stand at the head of the confessional tradition, but it also raises some fascinating questions in its relation to its unique cultural enclave. Obviously, much of the poignance of the *Journal* for both the author and the reader springs from the fact of the *passage* of the Quaker culture. Is it one of the ingredients of profound expression that it must originate in and convey the tension between dear arrest and painful transience in a cultural moment? Has it been the fate of the American artist from the beginning always to live, peculiarly to live, amid such tensions?

It becomes safer as well as more meaningful, then, not to say of Woolman's *Journal* that it tells, with a historical objectivity possible only to God, the "true" story of his life. Rather it presents, as a work of art, a Woolman whom the finally unknowable John created—a persona—living patterns of a life he also imagined (and so could select for us *and* so could himself perform in his time). It will not do to look for the *real* John Woolman in the *Journal*. It will not even do to look for him in Janet Whitney's thorough biography. No method a biographer can invent will release him from the necessity to imagine the person of his subject, select the meaningful details, etc. But all that leaves us free, finally, to confront the man of the *Journal* in our imaginations and see what he is and means.

Woolman imagined a hero for the *Journal* who was not, as often in modern confessions, an anti-hero but a man who so heroically sought the will of God and the spirit of Christ that he achieved the image of Christ and became a hero of humility. For almost any reader the personality which thus comes through will seem attractive; for many, immensely so. Here is a man who has learned not merely to suppress or subdue his egotism but to discipline it creatively. And it is a discipline of love, of harmony with life in nature and people, of sympathy with suffering, and of active, intelligent, inventive effort to relieve pain and vanquish injustice. Here, courage and lowliness, morality and sweetness, spiritual richness and simplicity are linked together in an unpretentious drama of the death and transfiguration of the ego. Whether or not the author was "really" like that, his invention of John Woolman was a marvelous creation.

That creation has seemed, and will continue to seem, appealing to hosts of readers. But there can be no denying that, exactly as he intended, Woolman's religion will stand as a crucial factor in the depth and entirety of his credibility, or acceptability, and thus of his impact. A Christian, or one susceptible to the Christian sentiment, must treasure Woolman; while his image and his drama remain at best simply appealing to one whose belief or sentiments are estranged from Woolman's religion. Nevertheless, for any reader responsive to Woolman, the other literary pleasures of the *Journal* will be added to the attraction of the personality.

As a "confession," Woolman's *Journal* exerts the magic of its prose fictional character. It tells the never-failing fascinations of someone else's life narrative, with intriguing glimpses into how the mysteries were for him, what the textures were of his experience, how things went within his life style. And, of course, cultural exotic and personal mystic that he was, Woolman's life style is strange and wonderful enough to possess even romantic appeal for some

readers. But most of all, the appeal of the unfolding
form of the *Journal* is that of intellectual, moral, and
spiritual drama. It is first a drama of becoming: the
cumulative development of Woolman's conviction—
a true faith to be lived upon and lived for, full of
vital options and pursued with an utter earnestness
of moral reality. It then becomes the drama of an
extraordinary career—God-intoxicated yet humane;
self-sacrificial until, in the foolishness of Christ, it
comes to the ultimate vision that "John Woolman is
dead"; yet with the incidents of an active life par-
alleling rising conviction until immediately and historically fateful victories are won in the marketplace
world of men.

One ends the *Journal* as Woolman composed it—
with a curious sense of incompleteness. The narrative is a broken column. There remains an open-
ended sense of unfulfillment quite modern in its
ironies of anticlimax, almost bathos. And one feels
that even the earliest editors were eager to add the
little sea and English journals (as perhaps Woolman
was to write them in a way he apparently wrote
nothing else) out of a sense of aesthetic need to
drive the drama on to resolution. And that too seems
to explain the need of editions from the beginning
to add the eyewitness accounts of Woolman's death
and the "Testimonies" of the Quaker meetings. Finally, the drama of the *Journal* so composed is that
of the paradoxical drama of the life of a saint which
is an imitation of Christ. In Yorkshire, for reasons
impenetrable, on a mission unclear, at an age still
potentially vigorous and with work unknowable yet
to do, John Woolman dies, apparently irrelevantly,
of smallpox. It is a death in harness and in the full
odor of sanctity. There is something genuinely

tragic in it because the world is deprived of true
goodness; there is mystery in it; there is at least the
paradox in it of full assurance that John Woolman
would not have had it otherwise. He had not only
composed but finally lived the life he had imagined.

Testimony as to the unique beauty of the style of
the *Journal* has, from Charles Lamb and William
Ellery Channing to the present, been continuous and
distinguished. Proper stylistic analysis of Woolman
will have to await more definitive treatment of the
editorial problems of his text. For the present it may
be useful to comment upon what appear (aside
from the genius of the author's inner ear) to have
been the sources of a style so often praised as the
ultimate in "limpidity." Actually, Woolman's is not
a perfectly transparent or "invisible" style. It has a
definite, and very attractive, voice of its own; and
the qualities of its sound and personality are more
marked in Mrs. Gummere's version of the manuscript than in the corruptly homogenized texts in
which Woolman has generally been read.

The sources of the style appear to be three: the
fine essay style of Woolman's eighteenth-century
predecessors and contemporaries, whom all sorts of
subtle colorations suggest that he knew better than
any ordinarily evidential methods of proof permit
one to claim; the living oral tradition of Quaker
"chanting" style preserved in meeting "openings"
(and preaching?) but suppressed by "overseers"
from Quaker publication; the notably plain but
rather dull official Quaker style. This multiplicity of
origins suggests that Woolman learned to make official Quaker style unobtrusively elegant and harmonious by blending it with Augustan ease when
he wished and that he knew how to adapt from the
oral tradition something of its prophetic and pulsat-

ing fire when he wished.[11] Whatever else it was, and Woolman's style cries out for extended, expert analysis, that style was a first-rate aesthetic achievement; it was anything but the performance of an "illiterate tailor."

IV

The *Journal* represented Woolman's larger mission —to the world outside the wavering boundaries of the old Quaker culture. So did the visit to Wyalusing. And the tug toward that mission appears to have been profoundly engaged in the painful time of troubles with which his life ended. Though nothing much is known objectively about the subject, Woolman's health apparently declined gradually after his "fever" in 1761. A valetudinarian note recurs in the *Journal* references to the succeeding years. And in 1769 there came a sort of crisis which

[11] A glance at the oft-erased and emended texts of the MSS would revise any opinion that Woolman was a mere "natural" or unconscious writer. For background on the whole stylistic-aesthetic problem see esp. F. B. Tolles, "The Quaker Esthetic," *Quakers and the Atlantic Culture,* pp. 73–90; D. Elton Trueblood, "The Career of Elias Hicks," *Byways in Quaker History,* pp. 88–93; Wright, p. 188, but most especially the ground-breaking essay by Jackson I. Cope, "Seventeenth Century Quaker Style," *PMLA,* September, 1956, pp. 725–54. I think every study of Woolman's style will have to begin with Professor Cope. In Woolman's case, I should hypothesize that Woolman's intense inward experience, his mysticism, led him to recapitulate the experience of the First Publishers and that he became accustomed to the verbal conduct of both his ministry and much of his subjective life in the "chanting" style of the early Quakers. Professor Cope identifies and illustrates that style and documents its suppression long before Woolman by censoring "overseers" and its replacement by an aggressively common-sensical plain style. He does not suggest the covert oral "in-group" survival of the "chanting" style; but I suspect there is good evidence of that survival. For evidence of Woolman's use of it, examine his rhetoric, especially in high exhortative moments; and for a clear case see his letter to Susanna Lightfoot, even the first paragraph (p. 150), in Omerod Greenwood, "John Woolman and Susanna Lightfoot: His Unpublished Letter to Her," *Friends Historical Society Journal,* XLVIII (1957), pp. 147–56.

was decisive at once intellectually, spiritually, and emotionally.

The impression one gets from the activities of Woolman's last quadrennium is that of a mind and spirit beating its wings to break out of confines into a larger sphere. Was it the sense of missions to be done before death, or a drive to wider fields than the local provinces, the constricted culture—or both and possibly more? Woolman not only wrote; he planned an expedition toward the heart of slavery and of the slave-exploiting trade of Quakerdom, the West Indies, perhaps Barbados.

This planning involved him in negotiations with and even testimonies against some of his best friends —Pembertons and Smiths—who were deep in the West Indies trade. Finally, "tossed as in a Tempest" with his conflicts, Woolman found that "Obedience" required him not to go, and he returned home still feeling "like a sojourner." Shortly afterward he fell ill of that self-diagnosed "pleurisy" from which he nearly died. Out of the "exercises" inwardly accompanying this agony came the sense of total spiritual arrival, fulfillment, and resignation expressed in his vision of the angelic song, *"John Woolman is dead."* In that same key he sounded the final notes of the *Journal* proper as he gathered up his collected manuscripts and placed them in the hands of John Pemberton before he left for England in 1772.

The stories of Woolman's voyage to England form some of the best-loved tales of his hagiography: Woolman in the steerage, Woolman first snubbed for his singularities and then accepted for his spirituality by the London Yearly Meeting, Woolman on foot through England pitying the tortured horses and postboys, Woolman dying in a style of courage and comfort forgotten by our century.

The aim of the voyage seems always to have been vague; Woolman simply felt called to it. Perhaps he was going in order to find out why he had to. The little journals of the sea voyage and the English experience and the five "last essays" done on shipboard show Woolman experimenting with variations on forms and ideas, expressing himself successfully but not otherwise freshly, and perhaps storing up materials for writings never finished. His wider mission was now to speak to the world fulfilling the role of the writer of *The Journal of John Woolman.*

Chapter VII

WOOLMAN'S IDEAS AND THE AMERICAN TRADITION

Now I find that in pure obedience the mind learns contentment in appearing weak and foolish to that wisdom which is of the world. . . . The natural man loveth eloquence, and many love to hear eloquent orations: and if there is not a careful attention to the gift men who have once labored in the pure gospel ministry, growing weary of suffering, and ashamed of appearing weak may kindle a fire, compass themselves about with sparks, and walk in the light,—not of Christ who is under suffering,—but of that fire which they, going from the gift, have kindled. And that in hearers, which is gone from the weak suffering state, into the worldly wisdom, may be warmed with this fire, and speak highly of these labors. . . .

Almost from the moment of his death Woolman began to be canonized in Quaker tradition. And with the publication of the two-volume "Works" in 1774—the *Journal* as Part I, *Other Writings* as Part II—that elevation became as official as it could ever be. The *Journal*, which has been continuously in print, took on the stature of a classic with the edition by John Greenleaf Whittier in 1871. It entered the *Harvard Classics* in 1909 and *Everyman's Li-*

brary in 1910 and is currently available in a number of forms. His lesser writings have been unevenly but rather frequently republished. None of that would have surprised Woolman, who appears to have planned just such communication with his sect. What he did not, probably could not, provide for was that he should now be looked toward for "ideas."

Indeed it is doubtful that Woolman could have admitted that he entertained or wielded "ideas." To himself he dealt in Truth, the revelations of God to a mind "under the cross." Nevertheless his ideas have relevance both historical and present to any student of the life of the mind in America. This relevance falls into three orders: the historical relevance of Woolman's relations with the mind of his own time; the historical relevance of his impact upon and his relations with the mind of the nearly two centuries since his death; and, with increasing momentousness in the current moment, the relevance and significance of Woolman's mind to this immediate day.

I

In the long-familiar story, the first colonists to set foot on the American Atlantic beaches with those prints in the easternmost sands planted a frontier— a place where the wilderness, the wild West, and the culture of European village-agrarian civilization met. As the early generations pushed the frontier back to the fall-line limits of tidewater (beyond which lay such typical horrors as "the terrible Lycoming wilderness" which Woolman penetrated as far as Wyalusing), the cultural units east of that limit, while still politically colonies, swiftly became culturally provinces. They began to develop provincial American cultures, cultures which took on characteristics different from the central, capitoline culture of England, and cultures which, behind barriers geographical, religious, and ethnic, became different from those of other provinces. Dammed behind the mountains, in a century of relative population immobility and sharply increasing prosperity, the American provincial cultures waxed dense and potent.

If the question, foreseen, of course, long before Emerson, whether there was ever to be an "American culture" were to be answered affirmatively, the answer would, then, have to come from those generally American yet intrinsically distinct provincial cultures. When would those cultures cease to be colonial? When they produced a life of the mind and imagination vital, however derivative, upon their own ground. When would they cease to be provincial? When they began, not to be "autochthonous," but to return to the grand concert of Western culture something fresh, stimulating, effective, and usable in exchange for all they got. That relationship would become precisely the relationship to Western culture of the European nations or provinces (as in Italy and Germany especially).

The American contribution began to come in the provincial era, before there was any United States of America. It began to come in many small, sometimes primitive ways; but it came most impressively in the art of letters and in the products of three extraordinarily interesting American minds: those of Franklin, Edwards, and Woolman.[1]

---

[1] For an earlier recognition of the significance of this triadic relationship, see Frank Davidson, "Three Patterns of Living," *AAUP Bulletin*, XXXIV (Summer, 1948), pp. 364–74.

Born less than three years after Edwards (1703), Franklin (1706) outlived him by an entire generation and Woolman by more than half that time (1790). Edwards, in turn, who was graduated from Yale in the year of Woolman's birth, died (1758) at the height of Woolman's powers. The three were contemporaries for thirty-eight years. Edwards and Woolman seem to corroborate the theory of Evelyn Underhill that mystics appear historically in waves following the great waves of energy, of integration of power, of social control and expression which mark what we call the major epochs of history. Though it would be foolish to overstress the neatness of the relation, the phenomenon of Edwards follows the grand New England integration during which Yankee culture first flowered upon the ruins of the theocratic utopia. Woolman came after the efflorescence of the Quaker culture upon the collapse of the "Holy Experiment."

In the long view it is much more important that Edwards and Woolman were mystics and creators than that they began by playing roles as radical reversionists toward the first impulses of their respective utopian heritages. As types of the mystic—and of the American mystic in his beginnings—they are worth detailed comparative study. Edwards' ecstasies in contemplation of God's unspoiled, gorgeous American nature (cp. "Personal Narrative" and *Images of Divine Things*) are more overtly fervid, if ultimately no deeper, than Woolman's. And it was Edwards who carefully defined the *identification*—not to be surpassed before Whitman—of Woolman and himself with life as "The Nature of True Virtue," as a wholly disinterested "love of being in general." In their mysticism, the individuality and inwardness independent of all sociality, there was something American. Not that either was lost to institutions. Edwards was gladly the priest of a church locked in forbidding traditions of discipline; and Woolman was from youth a Quaker's Quaker. Rather, the life which mattered and the life which created existed for both too inwardly and too upwardly. The necessary implication was that institutions exist to serve that life and at last only to serve it.

Woolman and Edwards thus became rebels by transcending through overfulfilling their traditions. But it is as instructive to look at their differences as at their similarities. As Fenimore Cooper, who had learned about it painfully at Yale, said, "They take the mind hard in New England." Nobody ever took it harder than Jonathan Edwards. Hence his formidable lifelong struggle to produce a *Summa Theologica* for his time and place, the achieved fragments of which have been so impressive. And thence the war in his mind, so modern, so American, between metaphysic and experience, head and heart, mind and man. The really significant difference between these two is not so much that "Sinners in the Hands of an Angry God" was impossible to Woolman, who has nothing to say about hell. To Woolman as to Emerson and all the Emersonians (including the Henry James of "The Beast in the Jungle") the terror of evil, the horror of sin, was their denial of being, their plunge into nothingness. The significant difference comes on one side from Woolman's frank dismissal of the formal intellect and on the other side from his affirmation of the possibility of ultimate goodness in the present, common life given man by God.

Triadically linked with Edwards and Franklin, then, Woolman represents a middle path between

Edwards' ecstatic, impossible transcendency and Franklin's triumphant worldliness. To say that is not to fall into the popular romantic game of Franklin-scorning. The marvel of Franklin is his supreme ability to see exactly and grasp firmly the "givens" of his world. To think him shallow, materialistically cynical, and personally or spiritually insignificant is to miss his ironies and be, perhaps a little unsophisticatedly, taken in by the Franklin personae of "The Way to Wealth," *The Autobiography,* and the bagatelles. As his "Articles of Faith and Acts of Religion," to cite only the key document, shows clearly, Franklin was neither irreverent, unspeculative, nor unbelieving. He was a man who had to go by sight; he saw only one world, but perhaps for that reason he saw it preternaturally well.

It is almost impossible to believe that Woolman and Franklin did not know each other and completely impossible to suppose that Franklin was not an imposing figure on the horizon of "the world" with which Woolman was engaged. Even had they been pleasant acquaintances, however, it is understandable that Franklin's name should not appear in the *Journal.* Woolman's autobiography had an aim quite different from memoirs of the type which it has been suggested should be entitled "Great Men Who Have Known Me." But to Woolman, Franklin must have been the very image, both personally and as projected in his writings, of the man of the world worldly.

Franklin not only seemed but was an entirely different kind of American. The ego-strong son of an immigrant shopkeeper, Franklin was never entangled in the hopes, however poignant, of a Heavenly City in the wilderness. Franklin escaped with joy into the toleration and opportunities of Pennsylvania. He navigated the lines of force of the provincial era with the skill of a born master and rode them to a bewildering series of triumphs. To a Woolman such a career must represent the perfection of "the spirit of fierceness." Franklin understood the vanities of the self, the mind, the world, and of power; but he accepted them with irony and enjoyed his mastery: what else was there for him to do? Woolman's lowliness, if Franklin ever knew it, must have seemed still another vanity—and not nearly so much fun as some others.

The conflict between the minds of Woolman and Franklin was irreconcilable except at one key point. Franklin lived long enough with his ironies to come to a worldly belief in the ethics of pity, mercy, and kindness—that secular *caritas*—which might have seemed to Woolman at least a halfway house, that virtue of the natural man to which Woolman often appealed, one certainly far superior to the spirit of fierceness. Franklin's, too, would be a permanent landmark for one way of the American mind.

There are ironies Franklin would in his way have enjoyed in the fact that Woolman and Edwards both fell victims to their age's endemic plague of smallpox. Woolman's sister died of the disease, and it was always on the horizon of his consciousness, as the *Journal* and his letters show. It was particularly the scourge of Americans visiting the comparatively crowded, metropolitan, and unsanitary England of Woolman's age.[2] A re-echoing colonial scandal arose from Edwards' death in 1758 after inoculation against smallpox. Whether Edwards died of his inoculation itself or of the aftereffects of inoculation—septicemia—he represented many whose inocula-

---

[2] See Gummere, "Introduction," *Journal*, pp. 56-7, *et passim*.

tions were at least as unhappy in effect as the disease they had hoped to avoid. And in the minds of both Franklin and Woolman the event must have aroused curious waves of response.

To the common-sense logic of "natural" psychology there is still, even in our incessantly "immunized" age, something unsettling about invading one's body with the poisons of a disease in order to forestall the same. But to the ages before Pasteur such practices smacked of necromancy or, at the very least, of Faustian gambles in the intellectual dark with inexplicable forces. Inoculation for smallpox (a very different thing from the later vaccination) became a bitter issue between enthusiasts for the new and "philosophic"—not then yet to be confused with "scientific" conservatives. As his brother James's apprentice in Boston, Franklin had helped carry on a loud fight of the liberal wits against the inoculating, blasphemous pedantries of Cotton Mather, who had taken the trouble to learn enough about the practice to introduce it to Boston. Later Franklin had become a firm supporter of inoculation, although his dear and only legitimate son, Francis (or "Franky"), had died, uninoculated, of smallpox in 1736.

Against this background, Woolman's eventual and painful death by smallpox, long after having, for examined considerations, declined to be inoculated, becomes significant. He joined himself with the long line of American minds which have been profoundly skeptical about the ultimate efficacy of reason. On mission tour in 1757, he lay under the stars meditating upon the harmonies of nature and the original consonance with them of Adam and Eve, whom God "by the Gracious Influence of his Spirit, Illuminated their understanding, and Shewed them what was Acceptable to Him, and tended to their true Felicity as Intelligent Creatures, did also provide means for their happy living in this world, as they attended to the manifestations of his Wisdom." And this led him to the next point, which was the consideration of man's "gift of Improving in things useful." Kept in harmony, that was certainly a "good Gift." But "Inventions of men" sought out "in the Creaturely Cunning and self-exaltation . . . as in the first motion it was evil, so the effects of it have been, and are evil."

In this light the spirit of Franklin's inventions and experiments must, on the whole, have been judged good. But, upon the dawning threshold of an age of technology, a rigorous test of values had been erected. Of its judgment of the labors of Eli Whitney, for instance, there could be little doubt.

Equally unsettling are the ideas upon which during a smallpox epidemic of 1759 Woolman declined to be inoculated. His principles are those of an organic, harmonious naturism. If there be disharmony in nature, that must come from an ultimately harmonious agency. One of Woolman's views is jeremiac: "I have looked on the Smallpox as a Messenger sent from the Almighty, to be an Assistant in the Cause of Virtue, and to incite us to consider whether we Employ our time only in such things as are Consistent with Perfect Wisdom and goodness." The disciplines of avoiding gadding about for frivolous reasons and of maintaining health practices are thus reinforced. Woolman denies that natural or catastrophic evils—earthquakes, wars, pestilences, famines—are accidental, capricious or, indeed, finally evil. They are salutary: ". . . where the kind Invitations and Gentle Chastisements of a Gracious God have not been attended to, his Sore Judge-ments have at times been poured out upon people."

Man's task, then, is to pay heed. Nevertheless, returning at last to the key question, Woolman finds it imaginable that there might be a proper resolution of the smallpox problem. He is not finally anti-intellectual or even antiscientific. He demands, as always, reason and method in harmony with God:

Had He Endowed man with understanding to hinder the force of this disease by innocent means, which had never proved mortal nor hurtful to our bodies, Such discovery might be considered as the period of chastisement by this distemper, where that Knowledge Extended. But as life and health are His gifts, and not to be disposed of in our wills, to take upon us, when in health, a distemper of which some die, requires great clearness of knowledge that it is our duty to do so.

A century after Woolman, John Greenleaf Whittier would see that final note as a prophetic call for vaccination—and by implication for the whole spectrum of modern immunological techniques. A century after Whittier, one may wonder if Woolman does not still "speak to the condition" of the mechanistic arrogance of a technological society which in serene ignorance threatens the entire fabric of nature to the agony, for instance, of the responsible ecologist. Franklin and Edwards, and many a twentieth-century observer, could readily have joined with Woolman in observing that "the human Mind is not naturally fortified with that Firmness in Wisdom and Goodness necessary to an independent Ruler" and that the assumption of "absolute Command" by "frail Men, in their own Wills, . . . hath a direct Tendency to vitiate their Minds. . . ."

II

Except in politics, to the American mind of the nineteenth century the riches of the eighteenth-century mind generally remained buried treasure. The Quakers were remembered by the democratic historians as vaguely apostles of freedom. For most of the rest, the latter century's feeling was summed up in Dr. Oliver Wendell Holmes's famous comic poem, "The Deacon's Masterpiece, or, 'the Wonderful One-Hoss-Shay.'" The mind of the provincial past seems quaint, a ludicrous antique creaking on miraculously until all at once it crumbles away and is gone forever from the face of a truly wonderful modernity. Only a quite external side note tells us that Holmes felt the Deacon's shay to be an objective correlative for the Calvinism of Jonathan Edwards.

John Woolman remained, of course, a living influence upon the antislavery movement and a vital presence (though in America not one efficacious against divisiveness) with the Quakerism of the first century after his death. Woolman was a hero to Elias Hicks, though Woolman might have found it hard to recognize his own image in that embattled, rather breezy Jacksonian Friend. Whether there was somehow an outreach from Woolman through Hicks to the impassioned empathy of Walt Whitman would seem to be one of those questions of diffused influence answerable by nothing better than intuition. In John Greenleaf Whittier's case, however, there is no doubt. Woolman was his childhood's prophet, his fighting abolitionist's stay, and

the saint of his latter years' devotion. Whittier introduced him to an enthusiastic William Ellery
Channing and early put him in his poems:

> . . . how passing lovely
>   Is the track of Woolman's feet!
> And his brief and simple record
>   How serenely sweet!
>
>   *   *   *   *   *
>
> Beauty, such as Goethe pictured,
>   Such as Shelley dreamed of, shed
> Living warmth and starry brightness
>   Round that poor man's head.
>
> Not a vain and cold ideal,
>   Not a poet's dream alone,
> But a presence warm and real,
>   Seen and felt and known.
>
> When the red right-hand of slaughter
>   Moulders with the steel it swung,
> When the name of seer and poet
>   Dies on Memory's tongue,
>
> All bright thoughts and pure shall gather
>   Round that meek and suffering one,—
> Glorious, like the seer-seen angel
>   Standing in the sun! [3]

Thus the early Whittier in the swinging measures
of hymnody which often seem Quaker-incongruous
in his verse. The late Whittier, marking the end of
the first century of Woolman's *Journal* in the world

---

[3] From "To ———, with a Copy of Woolman's Journal" (1840),
Poetical Works, IV, pp. 20–1.

by editing it into fixture as a classic, saw in it the solution of the notorious Victorian Dilemma. In 1870, at a moment fateful for it, Whittier wrote to and of "The Society of Friends," predicting the hour "when under the searching eye of philosophy and the terrible analysis of science, . . . the doctrine of the Holy Spirit, as proclaimed by George Fox and lived by John Woolman, shall be recognized as the only efficient solvent of doubts raised by an age of restless inquiry." [4]

Whittier was unique in his times: a recognized poet and a Quaker in good standing. And he was a child and then a poet of the age—after his fashion, in short, a romantic poet. Therefore his was, as Rufus Jones pointed out, a mind "essentially in the Platonic stream" with profound debts, direct and indirect, to Samuel Taylor Coleridge.[5] Whittier was thus much moved to discover that Lamb and his circle, especially Henry Crabb Robinson but including Coleridge himself, were enthusiasts of the *Journal*. He quoted Lamb's essay "A Quaker's Meeting" repeatedly: "Get the writings of John Woolman by heart, and love the early Quakers."

On the American side of this same romantic-Platonic drift, part idealism, part sentimentality, there was great interest in Quakerism, especially among the Transcendentalists. Emerson, for all the self-consciousness of his rebellious modernity, felt a deep kinship. Early in his career he was asking, "Did you ever meet a *wise Quaker?* They are few, but a sublime class of speculators. They have been perhaps the most explicit teachers of the highest article to which human faith soars [:] the strict

---

[4] "The Society of Friends," *Prose Works*, III, p. 313.

[5] "Whittier's Fundamental Religious Faith," in *Byways in Quaker History*, pp. 26–7.

union of the willing soul to God and so the soul's access at all times to a verdict upon every question which the opinion of all mankind cannot shake and which the opinion of all mankind cannot confirm." [6] That is an effective summary of John Woolman in one aspect. It is an equally effective summary in the same aspect of the greatest of Emerson's own disciples and successors, Henry David Thoreau.

The significances of the parallels of Thoreau and Woolman are inescapable. Both lived lives of intense and not infrequently mystic inwardness. Both found it necessary to shape their outward lives as testimonies and examples—if not rebukes—to their times. Both created masterpieces in the same special—and perhaps specially American—literary genre. And each, in his way, appears now to have lived most significantly as the expressive genius of a basic human condition, the same variety of religious experience: the state of the saintly soul at war with spiritual sloth.

Between the "actual" lives of Woolman and Thoreau and the autobiographies as imagined and presented exists the same disproportion between the struggling, often failing, inevitably *queer* person and the figure implied by the nobility of the work and the beauty of the persona upon which the work is founded. The well-known case of Thoreau helps one to see that this disproportion is necessary to the artist and that Woolman is one with Thoreau as the type of the mystic-rebel-isolato-artist. It is necessary that the maker be far more contingent, flawed, anxious, confused, and often mistaken than the figure of the fiction which represents the high-

[6] To Benjamin Peter Hunt, January 23, 1835. *The Letters of Ralph Waldo Emerson*, ed. Ralph L. Rusk (New York: Columbia University Press, 1939), I, p. 433.

est reach of a disciplined imagination. In the long run it has been saddeningly destructive of the truths Woolman and Thoreau both spent themselves to hint at that their disciples and admirers have been disturbed by the difference between person and persona.

If *Walden* and the *Journal* are triumphs of the art of fiction, "On the Duty of Civil Disobedience" and Woolman's set of "Considerations" remind us that on the line from Woolman through Thoreau lies the development of an American tradition of absolute religious radicalism. What is American about this tradition is perhaps, again, its individualism, its stark confrontation of the soul with light and then of the enlightened soul with society. Attacking slavery and all the complicit, hypocritical webs of social sin and horror beneath and around that institution, Woolman and Thoreau were at one in seeing that the important fact was not so much the darkness of the sin as the absolute, aboriginal spiritual value of the slave. The offense against that value necessitated every lawful effort, including simple rejection of the moral authority of a persistently immoral society, to assert human value and abolish the offense.

But in seeing these fundamental likenesses between Woolman and Thoreau, one is led immediately to notice basic differences. Thoreau's touchy pride, his obvious intellectual and spiritual arrogance, his notorious incapacity for normal emotional contacts, and the personally competitive hostilities which grew upon him have raised psychiatric speculations in the present century. Though Woolman and Thoreau shared the outcast state of social eccentrics, some of Thoreau's characteristics stand in sharp contrast to Woolman's humility, warmth,

sweetness, and irenism.[7] Woolman, of course, long
enjoyed that support of a culture and home which
Thoreau lacked and yearned for. Thoreau's favorite
trope for himself—the myth of Apollo in the menial
service of King Admetus—could never have occurred
to Woolman's consciousness. But even when Woolman had outgrown his failing culture and become a
sojourner with his family, he retained something
Thoreau in the end desperately lost. To the finish
Woolman's religion worked for him: Thoreau's
failed.

The *Journal* was capped at last with the testimonies of Woolman's holy dying. The author's life
fulfilled, confirmed, and finally conformed to his
work. *Walden,* by far the more brilliant work of art,
closes with the cry of Chanticleer: "There is more
day to dawn." But every Thoreauvian knows that
less, not more, day dawned in the author's mind and
work thereafter. In the context of time as well as in
Thoreau's life after *Walden* the lesson of the book
is that Thoreau was trying by vain bugling to blow
the light up the sky, not announcing the dawn. It
was more night—of doubt, anxiety, and the inability
to experience the confirming bursts of mystic glory
in nature any longer—which closed about him. And
this darkening of view was in the main trend of
American experience from the middle of the nineteenth century forward. Whitman's major prose effort to bugle up the sun, *Democratic Vistas,* with the
divine Literatus as its hero-persona, would look
toward long vistas of time before the full arrival of
the light. The next great example in the Woolman-

---

[7] Cp. Whittier's comment, "With nothing of [Thoreau's] scorn,
[Woolman] had all of Thoreau's commiseration, for people who went
about bowed with the weight of broad acres and great houses on
their backs." Whittier, ed., *Journal,* 92 n.

Thoreau genre, *The Education of Henry Adams,* crossing from the nineteenth to the twentieth century, would conclude that from neither history nor anywhere else could come the rays to lighten the chaos of modern multiplicity.

III

From the midst of that multiplicity John Woolman has been seen to be primarily significant as a prophet of social relations. With his ironies Socratically self-directed, or unconscious, or conscientious, or conciliatory, Woolman has seemed a more viable prophet of economic responsibility than Thorstein Veblen—and at least as revolutionary. But that appearance, again as in the nineteenth century, has been largely in the camps of Quakerism.[8] Even Vida Scudder, introducing her edition of the *Journal,* found it necessary to scold and scorn Woolman a bit for his lack of Marxist revolutionary optimism: an innocent perspective of 1910 not without its pathos a bitter half-century later.

But perhaps the most interesting of twentieth-century perspectives upon John Woolman was that of Theodore Dreiser. Of Dreiser the artist it has been said with a certain hyperbolic truth that he possessed genius but no talent. Every candid study of his life and thought shows him to have been in the ordinary senses of logic and consistency a man of extraordinarily confused mind. Yet his power as an artist is undeniable. The vigor of his probing into the human condition in the first half of our century remains compelling. And from his attraction toward

---

[8] See Reginald Reynolds, *The Wisdom of John Woolman* (London: G. Allen & Unwin, 1948); and *John Woolman and the 20th Century* (Wallingford: Pendle Hill Pamphlets, 1958), for examples.

Quakerism generally and John Woolman in particular came one of Dreiser's most humane and appealing novels, *The Bulwark*.

The Bulwark was the book Dreiser was almost always more or less writing, for it was to have been the book in which imaginatively he resolved the religious gropings which stirred in him through a strangely checkered lifetime.[9] Perhaps as early as 1910 Dreiser had conceived the idea of an ironic novel on the familial and financial disasters of a pretentiously "good" man, a Quaker, whose biblical rigors proved life-destroying. For years Dreiser touted the book to publishers and wrote inchoate versions, only to lay it aside for World War I, another book, a creative block, World War II. Finally he "finished" it by main force of permitting friends and publishers' editors to try and reconcile conflicting versions as best they could. In the meantime, of course, Dreiser's always veering thought had traversed further and further from the muddled Darwinism of *Hey Rub-a-Dub-Dub* toward the muddled mystical holism of the never-published work on philosophy which occupied most of his last years.

Just why Dreiser should have made Solon Barnes, the protagonist of *The Bulwark*, a Quaker to begin with is not clear, unless it was simply as a cover for an intended portrait of Dreiser's own father, a devout and rigorous Catholic. Nor is it clear just when Woolman entered the picture. Dreiser might easily have been introduced to him by his friend

---

[9] For general background on *The Bulwark* see Robert H. Elias, *Theodore Dreiser: Apostle of Nature* (New York: Alfred A. Knopf, Inc., 1949); and Elias, ed., *Letters of Theodore Dreiser* (Philadelphia: University of Pennsylvania Press, 1959), *passim;* Helen Dreiser, *My Life with Dreiser* (Cleveland: World Publishing Co., 1951), esp. p. 80.

Llewellyn Powys, who had published an admiring essay [10] on Woolman at a time when *The Bulwark* was much in Dreiser's thought. He had certainly been reading Elias Hicks (or about him) around 1927.[11] But as Gerhard Friedrich has shown,[12] the most direct impact of Woolman on Dreiser came through the mediation of Woolman's major Quaker disciple of the generation after Whittier, Rufus Jones.

Professor, philosopher, historian, diplomat, humanitarian, mystic, leading Friend of his time, and ecumenical statesman, Jones possessed a reality, depth, and weight of personality worthy of the finest in Quaker tradition and was cultivated as perhaps no Quaker could ever have been before him. Dreiser met Jones through joint efforts to bring relief to sufferers in the Spanish Civil War during 1938 and was so deeply impressed that he began at once to read Jones's books, especially the autobiographical ones. Having learned how profoundly Jones was indebted to Woolman, Dreiser also bought and carefully marked a copy of the Whittier edition of the *Journal*. He not only repeatedly "saw" Solon Barnes in the *Journal*, he plagiarized Jones's own memoir at several points, and finally built the resolution of the novel around quotations of Woolman's visions of the mystic light accompanied by *"Certain evidence of Divine Truth"* and of the angelic lay *"John Woolman is dead."* He even at this climactic moment lifted passages from Whittier's introduction to the *Journal*.[13]

---

[10] In *Thirteen Worthies* (New York, 1923).

[11] Elias, *Theodore Dreiser: Apostle of Nature*, p. 261.

[12] See esp. "Theodore Dreiser's Debt to Woolman's *Journal*," *American Quarterly*, VII (Winter, 1955), 385–92.

[13] In addition to Friedrich, see Elizabeth Gray Vining, *Friend of Life. The Biography of Rufus M. Jones* (Philadelphia: J. B. Lippincott Co., 1958), pp. 20–1, 28–9, 266–7.

After reading *The Bulwark*, Rufus Jones was correct in complaining that, by the best ordinary stand-
ards, it was hardly a novel, that the characters were
undramatized lay figures, that Dreiser had never
grasped the essence of the Quaker family or meeting, and (with an evident philosopher's silent con-
tempt for the quality of the ideas) that it was all
just a platform for "the author's theories." [14] More
professionally literary critics had been saying the
same things and worse—and correctly—for many
years without getting at the secret of Dreiser's obviously crude literary power. Certainly it was not
the quality of the thought behind the "theories."
In introducing *The Living Thoughts of Thoreau*,
1939, while directly engaged with Woolman, Dreiser
had found in Thoreau, not very keenly, ". . . these
two beliefs (1) that solitary contemplation of nature
brought a harmony with the spiritual force which
created the world, and (2) that what is right is so
by intuition. Of course, John Foxe [*sic*] had that
thought. . . . Also John Woolman, whom, in many
of his solitary communion deductions, Thoreau re-
sembles. Also Buddha, Jesus, and Lao-Tze." Listing
again Diogenes, Christ, Buddha, St. Francis,
Thomas à Kempis, John Huss, "John Foxe," John
Bunyan, and Woolman in a fine syncretistic scram-
ble, Dreiser reached for a pinnacle in characterizing
Thoreau's peers:

> All these men were arrested by the beauty
> and the mystery of life, the joy and the pain,
> the ignorance and the wisdom, the good and
> the evil, the birth and the death. And each
> seeking to find something above technical

[14] *Ibid.*, p. 29.

structures in life to solve the orphaned ache of one who is not ready to believe that for all his ills or grievances or longings, he is to be dismissed at death, with death. A sad tale, mates! [15]

The qualities of style in either writing or thinking are not necessarily higher in *The Bulwark* or any other Dreiser novel. Writers are almost never good philosophers, however, and literary success has often been achieved in spite of shoddy style. In the end Dreiser's power over a reader's imagination seems to come from the sheer weight of his concentration upon himself and his yearnings, his emotions—concerning which his characters and their experiences are only ways of talking. Dreiser mesmerizes us in spite of all his faults into concentrating and ultimately caring intensely with him about his emotions.

What Woolman provided Dreiser was, in short, a means of resolving at the end (*The Bulwark* was published posthumously) his own lifelong tensions of personality with power, wealth, and destiny. In Dreiser's time his was supremely the representative voice of the American watching with anguish and fascination the rise of incredible new structures of power and alternately elated and terrified by his prospects of rising with or being crushed by them. In the history of Solon Barnes, Dreiser had originally meant to tell another version of the mechanistic tragedy of pathetic irony ("A sad tale, mates!") and to show the futilities of orthodox "goodness" and faith. But in Woolman, Jones, and Whittier he saw another light—even if it was not the Quaker light.

---

[15] Theodore Dreiser, *The Living Thoughts of Thoreau* (London: Longmans, Green and Co., 1939), pp. 7, 8.

True to original plan, the bulk of Solon Barnes's life consists of reduction and retreat from childhood security and faith in rural Maine to prosperity in rather hypocritical Philadelphia banking and increasing emptiness of life despite a Puritanic sternness of morality. In the end that emptiness betrays Solon. His children are lured away from his bleakness toward the excitements of the world and are corrupted, his son destroyed. His banking connection with peculating partners severed, his wife dead of grief, his daughters confused and estranged, Solon is brought to the end Dreiser had so long ago foreseen. But at the last there is the turn which the earlier Dreiser could not have given to his feelings or the novel.

In one crucial scene, shaken Solon Barnes is made aware of his unity with nature and with the "Creative Force," or "Creative Divinity" which had designed all in beauty and, despite all tragedy, love. Putting it in his own terms, Solon comes to "thank God for this revelation of His universal presence and His good intent toward all things." And, outgrowing his old, stiff moralism, he sees "the need of love towards all created things." This scene Dreiser modulates into the climactic one centered upon reading Woolman's *Journal* by the artistically awkward and intellectually deliberately blurring device of shifting the point of view rapidly from that of Solon to that of his newly reconciled daughter Etta. Reading Woolman aloud to Solon, Etta feels suddenly illuminated by its "spiritual beauty." Herself spiritually sick of passion for an artist who had completely aroused and then deserted her because her passion threatened him creatively, she now begins to understand "a Love that first turned to God and thence spread out over all people and things

. . . to the poor, the weak, the slaves, the miners. . . . In this love and unity with all nature, as she now sensed, there was nothing fitful or changing or disappointing. . . . It was an ultimate relation to the very heart of being." [16]

Religiously Dreiser thus managed a rather neat syncretistic trick, despite the awkwardness of his means. He picked out from the heart of Woolman's vision something which blended well with his own doctrines without quite encountering Woolman's Christianity. As almost always with Dreiser's success, then, much of the power of *The Bulwark* inheres in a very lifelike open-endedness; and one is left not knowing how much of that indeterminacy stems from mere confusion and how much from the dark wisdom of an intense preconscious mind.

Left obscure among all this are Dreiser's intentions with regard to Woolman's economic thought. With no relation to his way of life as a successful writer, Dreiser's socioeconomic concerns during the last twenty years or so of his life were determinedly radical; and at the end of his life he joined the Communist Party for reasons which, in the historical context, seem incredibly romantic and ill-informed. He could not have failed to notice that Woolman had been a trenchant critic of the business mind and the economic aspects of "the spirit of fierceness." Perhaps Woolman's agrarianism put Dreiser off. It is not likely that Woolman's concerns against the uses of wealth for power over others, or for vanity and conspicuous consumption, abashed Dreiser. Perhaps he felt that the point had been made by the fable of Solon and the bank. If

---

[16] *The Bulwark* (New York: Doubleday & Co., Inc., 1946), pp. 316–19; 327–31.

so, it is doubtless fortunate that he did not undertake to syncretize Woolman's ideas with those of
the late Iosif Vissarionovich Dzhugashvili (Stalin).

IV

To consider Theodore Dreiser, however, is to
recognize that, although anxiously "modern" and
representing much that was modernist, he is anything but contemporary. He belongs to an era of
the past. And in the immediate present John Woolman has assumed a significance greater than ever
before. He is both a direct ancestor of, and a voice
directly relevant to, the fateful drive toward racial
justice in the America which seeks now to dispel the
cloud of historical guilt Woolman saw gathering
two centuries ago.

If not literally, it was certainly symbolically true,
as Whittier said, that Woolman's vision of terrible
historical calamity visited upon posterity for the sins
of slavery was borne out by the Civil War. Of all
the myriad commentators, perhaps none more eloquently and incisively than William Faulkner expressed Woolman's sense of the disabling guilt, both
North and South, for slavery which discharged the
tragic potential of the War. Many critics have remarked on the shaping of Faulkner's work by that
sense of historic guilt; and it came to final expression in the brooding commentary interlarded into
the self-edited and carefully rethought stories, central to Faulkner's imagination, of *Big Woods,* 1955.

But Faulkner's too is a mind of the past. And one
turns from him to shocks, sometimes shudders, of
recognition of new light on the questions of Woolman as well as Faulkner in the works of two minds
very much of the present—both American Negro

minds—those of Martin Luther King, Jr., and James Baldwin. It is quite imaginable that a future historian might say that, all unprepared in the glare of the nuclear crisis of the human race and of the global crises of ideological warfare and social revolution, it was said to America: "This night is thy soul required of thee." And the voice of God was the voice of the American Negro. A contemporary John Woolman might easily experience such a vision. And, indeed, James Baldwin, a half-hipster Jeremiah, has communicated such a vision, shot through with true and Manichean-sounding paradoxes, in *The Fire Next Time,* 1963.

Despite the variances in temperament and point of view of Baldwin and King, the unity of their experience and aims is striking. As a writer Baldwin is perhaps necessarily both self-educated and in the context of our times something of an *artiste-aliéné.* King is a leader-doer, a Ph.D. familiar with the frontiers of the theology which has newly become intellectually relevant, even exciting. King is profoundly *engagé,* and probably subject to the temptations normal to the intellectual enmeshed in politics. Estranged from the disastrous Fundamentalism of his adolescence yet still yearning for religion, Baldwin writes a moving sermon whose structural disconnections reflect and express the post-Freudian confusions which affect us all. Intellectually secure in theologically structured ideas, King writes in the great treatise-like tradition of the apology, as in his prophetic epistle to the ministers of the city written from Birmingham jail.[17] Actually *The Fire Next Time* and King's *Stride Toward Freedom: The Montgomery Story,* 1958,

---

[17] See "The Negro Is Your Brother," *The Atlantic Monthly,* 212 (August, 1963), pp. 78–88.

are works in the memoir-as-prophetic-gesture genre of Woolman's *Journal.* Yet it is striking that, for all the obvious intellectual culture of both, neither King nor Baldwin seems aware of the existence of Woolman or, what is perhaps more to the point, of the historical depths of the American traditions of thought and sentiment which Woolman represents and has in part authorized or inspired.

To point out that King and Baldwin ignore Woolman is, in the context of such a book as this, neither to complain of ignorance nor to charge that here are heirs to a paternity they forget. Neither Baldwin nor King quite needs John Woolman. King has Christ and the prophets, the Church Fathers and the heroes of Protestantism, Socrates, Jefferson, Lincoln and Thoreau, Gandhi and all the latest theologians. Baldwin has the artist-assimilated background of a reading clearly wide and often existentialist. The object here is of course to claim for Woolman a relevance to that fateful searching of the contemporary mind which King and Baldwin represent —a relevance and a significance John Woolman clearly possesses. And to say that is, finally, to accept in essentials exactly what Baldwin and King are saying to the conscience of our time as Woolman said it to the conscience of two centuries past: the Negro is a man, a brother; only a selfish love of misused power keeps us from knowing these facts; and the consequences of failing to act according to the truth are personally, spiritually, socially, and historically blasting.

ENVOI

Where Customs contrary to pure Wisdom
are transmitted against them; then I often feel
tender Compassion toward a young Generation,
and Desires that their Difficulties may not be
increased through Unfaithfulness in us of the
Present Age.

From the beginning John Woolman's reputation
has suffered from sentimentalization. Even the
epistles from Yorkshire recording his holy dying
have a touch of saccharine, and the rather windy
poetry which celebrated him, before Whittier, alternated between the sentimental and the false sublime. As close to Woolman's death as December
17, 1772, one George Mason exploited the news to
show how one might be at once a loyal Quaker and
a genteel Man of Feeling with a nice command of
elegant variation. Mason informs "S. and D. Morris"
that he prays ". . . with comfortable Breathings for
your Preservation in that meek and lowly Faith
where our steps are Beautiful, our Conversation
adorned, our Conduct made amiable . . . and the
channel of pure Sympathetick Union kept open";
and he assures them that upon hearing "of our dear
Brother John Woolman's release" he "had bedew'd
his precious Memory with calm gentle Tears." [1]
Against such a background one understands Charles
Brockden Brown more readily.

In a sentimental age the image of Woolman the

---

[1] Original in Historical Society of Pennsylvania.

simple soul in primitive contact with God and nature, breathing out pure love and spiritual beauty from an utter and unconscious sainthood, became widely propagated. Brissot de Warville, Henry Crabb Robinson, Charles Lamb, even William Ellery Channing reflected the image. It is the basis of the standard textbook clichés about Woolman; even modern biographers have not been free of it. "In sentence after sentence, this common colonial tailor reveals a refinement of nature, a gentleness of conscience, a sanctity of thought . . . the direct, unaffected goodness of the simple man," said Llewellyn Powys with just a touch of English public school astonishment at what he was saying. The trouble, of course, is that this is the image of a plaster saint. It is too simple, too perfect, too abstract, too far removed from the confusions, contingencies, troubles, and sins of men.

There really arises a question, however, after sentimentality is barred and Woolman is seen struggling with his world and his psyche to live and to create. The question is whether Woolman has not made himself unavailable by compressing life and so his relationships to it into a presently useless oversimplification. The problem is there in Woolman's withdrawal from his culture. If one enjoys the benefits of a culture, may he dissociate himself from its sin and the consequences of it? The problem, especially for our times, is there in Woolman's agrarianism, his recoil from the city and his Early American illusion of "competence" for a small and virtuous because simplistic rural population. For many people the problem is there in Woolman's too-simple pacifism: suppose the Senecas *had* come on unchecked at the frontier?

These are all problems subsidiary to the main

question: can we dare to go to the roots of any moral or spiritual issue in our time, or are we too frightened, too drugged with indulgence, too selfish? It is revealing to have Sir Charles Percy Snow, the famous initiator of the latest squabble over modern multiplicity, addressing a huge ceremonial gathering in words John Woolman would applaud:

> We have got to fall back with great simplicity on the fact that the essence of each human person is equivalent to the essence of each other human person. . . . Unless we hold . . . patiently . . . that the essence of human beings is more important than their politics, their color, their race, hold that the resemblances between each of us are incomparably more important than the differences, then there is no hope for us. But there is much if we hold absolutely fanatically to that firm and simple faith.[2]

Snow's is one way of confronting another problem central to our time—the problem of making any sort of sense out of life by the inescapable way of choosing to have faith in something simple enough for viable belief. This is still that last question of Henry Adams: can the complex, pluralistic mind, confronted by change accelerating into multiplicity at a rate of geometric proportion, leap to cope with its challenges? Or must it be sullenly defeated? Or shall it accept limitations and so simplicities as its only hope of human survival?

To such problems John Woolman is obviously not irrelevant. Nor, to return to an earlier point, is he irrelevant to the great internal struggle of the

[2] "Three Dragons to Slay," *Michigan Alumnus,* LXIX (July, 1963), p. 317.

American soul over racism at this moment. The
spirit and the logic of the Rev. Mr. King are exactly
those of John Woolman, sectarianism aside and in
the perspective of two centuries since. The case of
Mr. Baldwin is fascinatingly varied. Attacked by a
Calvinism partly temperamental and partly an
anachronism from his youthful religiosity, he is prey
to a despair "black" in three senses: it is Negro in
point of view, it is faithless, it is charged full of bile.
And yet Baldwin wills himself to believe and not to
hate, to prophetically see "the white man" and
white America in the condition of Noah—to arch
out the rainbow of his fire-tested humanity and say:
". . . end the racial nightmare, and achieve our
country, and change the history of the world." Failing this, *the fire next time!* [3] Though King in his
spirit of "nonviolent resistance" is closer to the
whole Woolman than Baldwin, still it was precisely
the just arousal of "the spirit of fierceness" in the in-
jured victim which Woolman understood to be the
profoundest historic threat to the people vain with
power. That is the point of a subsidiary portion of
his greatest vision:

> I was then carried to the mines, where poor
> Oppressed people were digging rich treasures
> for those called Christians, and heard them
> blaspheme the name of Christ, at which I was
> grieved for His Name to me was precious.
> Then I was informed that these heathen were
> told that those who oppressed them were fol-
> lowers of Christ; and they said amongst them-
> selves: If Christ directed them to use us in
> this Sort then Christ is a cruel tyrant.

[3] *Op. cit.*, pp. 119–20.

Such attitudes, their unique literary expression, and their life expression in the conduct of an acute, effective reformer, merit such an accolade as that of Alfred North Whitehead: "Neither the Catholics, nor the Methodists, gave the first modern formulation of an explicit purpose to procure the abolition of slavery. This supreme honour belongs to the Quakers, and in particular to that Apostle of Human Freedom, John Woolman." [4] There are most legitimate kinds of heroes different from Woolman, kinds not dreamed of in his philosophy—heroes of the earth earthy and the world worldly, heroes of human pride and valor, even of the spirit of fierceness. But Woolman himself was more than just the model of meekness and empathy, of humility, simplicity, and redemptive suffering, of reconciliation and peacemaking. In his way he came bringing a sword, too. As George Macaulay Trevelyan put it on the eve of World War I, the antislavery movement arrived "in the nick of time," just before industrialization "could universalize the slave system." Woolman and his companions saved the world from an absolute infamy. And, said Trevelyan in oft-quoted words, there is historically a justification for Woolman's sense of the vengeances of time: "Close your ears to John Woolman one century, and you will get John Brown the next, with Grant to follow." [5] In our world of speeding change, Woolman—and King and Baldwin—are Jeremiahs to listen to.

In the end, no matter what one says, it seems impossible to evade the indictment King and Bald-

---

[4] *Adventures in Ideas* (New York: The Macmillan Co., 1933), pp. 28–9.

[5] *Clio, A Muse and Other Essays* (London: Longmans, Green and Co., 1914), pp. 141–2.

win—and Woolman—bring against our country's history and present condition. The question then becomes not whether to agitate our guilt but where to seek means of reformation. King would say, seek them in the great traditions of the best mankind has thought and found through the ages. Baldwin would say, create them radically new out of the naked despair of our culture's orphaned desolation. What Woolman in effect says is that there exist native roots, hidden American traditions, from which to draw the vital sap of cultural creativity.

Quite like a modern man, Woolman lived from relatively tranquil, simple times into complex, difficult violent, confusing times changing at bewildering rates of acceleration—and tried to come to terms with them and his sense of doom. A "Quaker Socrates," [6] his life and ideas are not separable. They were assimilated organically the ones to the other with that perfection we often enviously suggest when we yearn for "wholeness." This is the more true because his was an examined life, one which came under discipline to be lived as an *exemplum*. And it seems still the more true because most of what it is possible for us to know about the life and the ideas we know through Woolman's expression of his own vision of wholeness. Life, ideas, and expression from an organic continuum. And that is exactly as Woolman would have had it. No philosopher, he wished for life, not analysis, for significant act and expression, not a bloodless dance of categories.

Nevertheless his ideas are there. Precisely because they inform the life and writing to what becomes in our perspective a single work of primitive American art, yet art of living moral significance,

---

[6] *Ibid.*, p. 136.

John Woolman rewards our present contemplation. He does, in Quaker parlance, "speak to our condition." He is most valuable as a type-figure of one peculiarly beautiful and hopeful variation of the spirit of man in mystic and saintly affirmation. And for Americans he provides a focus of thought highly significant as an ingredient in our culture—the radical Quaker. Whether or not the Quakers have been the keepers of the American conscience, John Woolman is one of those who demonstrates that there has been a conscience to keep. He stands at the head of one major variant of the American conscience. And it is of no small worth in the present moment to remember that we have conscientious traditions. Most obviously we have a need not only for the assurance of the legitimacy of those traditions but a need to call them to vigorous new life in our individual beings and the life of the nation.

In the end there is a significance to John Woolman's ideas to which the question of Christian belief or unbelief is not relevant. The question he asks has been asked before and since. It has been given new vitality by Hungarians fighting against tanks in the streets, by Peace Corpsmen, and by jails full of Negro demonstrators. The question is, except as we give ourselves away, how shall we survive? "The worldly hope men set their hearts upon/ Turns ashes," says all the cumulated wisdom of the world. In the latest stage of composing his letter to the world, Woolman recorded the climactic vision of the angelic voice chanting, *"John Woolman is dead."* Yet he is paradoxically not dead—as he was, in still another paradox, not then dead except, as he interpreted the vision, dead in ego. Almost two hundred years after, Woolman is living in a world of which no vision, however fantastic, could have forewarned him.

Echoes from generation to generation of his work and word pulse, now fatefully amplified, in American life. The *Journal* stands, increasingly known, enticing readers wherever plain English, beautiful with the sounds of a truly speaking human voice, is read. In the strangely mixed and moving company of Franklin's *Autobiography, Walden, Democratic Vistas,* and *The Education of Henry Adams,* John Woolman's *Journal* belongs to American scripture. In connections like this it is well to remember that the United States belong to us alone; but America, though we may be its custodians, belongs to mankind.

SELECTED BIBLIOGRAPHY

This is not intended as a record of all the "sources consulted." Rather, it is a list of the references to which the student of Woolman would be particularly well advised to look for further investigation on his own. The two principal sources of manuscript materials relating to Woolman lie in the collections of the Historical Society of Pennsylvania and the Swarthmore College Friends Historical Library, both of which, along with almost all other sources, have been thoroughly exploited by the Mrs. Gummere and Whitney (*infra*). Cp. Joseph Jones, *et al.*, *American Literary Manuscripts*. Austin: University of Texas Press, 1960.

The Journal of John Woolman. With an Introduction by John G. Whittier. Boston: J. R. Osgood and Co., 1871.

This was the edition, compounding dozens of cumulative textual corruptions with the poet's emendations, which elevated the *Journal* to the status of a "classic." It was reprinted in at least fifteen impressions and has remained the base for popular editions to this day. Includes (without attribution) portions of William Tuke's letter describing John Woolman's last illness and death; in "Appendix" includes "The Testimony of the Friends in Yorkshire . . . ," "A Testimony of the Monthly Meeting of Friends in Burlington . . . ," and "A Word of

Remembrance and Caution to the Rich [A *Plea for the Poor*]." Whittier's notes are valuable and his introduction is both a Woolman and a Quaker *locus classicus*.

GUMMERE, AMELIA MOTT (ed.). *The Journal and Essays of John Woolman, Edited from the Original manuscripts with a Biographical Introduction by Amelia Mott Gummere*. Rancocas edition. New York: The Macmillan Co., 1922.

Great intelligence, years of devoted work, and the profit of extraordinary inside knowledge and contacts went into this landmark work of a gifted amateur. Not always consistent or accurate, the text, taken from manuscripts wherever possible, restored hundreds of original Woolman readings. Includes *Some Considerations on the Keeping of Negroes, Part I; Part II; Considerations on Pure Wisdom* . . . ; "Serious Considerations on Trade"; *A Plea for the Poor; Considerations on the True Harmony of Mankind;* "An Epistle"; *Last Essays*. The long and authoritative (if sometimes inchoate) "Biographical Sketch" reprints almost all known Woolman letters and other basic documents. It and the long appendix are rich mines of information. The bibliography is still the best available. Altogether, the indispensable Woolman reference.

WHITNEY, JANET (ed.). *The Journal of John Woolman*. Chicago: H. Regnery Co., 1950.

The most reliable and most readable text available. Returning from Mrs. Gummere to the manuscripts, Woolman's biographer has edited her informed version of a "clear text" (cp. Chapter VI, n. 7, *supra*). Includes the Yorkshire and Burlington "Testimonies," two letters from Edith Tuke in addition to the traditional letter from William Tuke on Woolman's death, and "Biographical Notes" streamlined down from Mrs. Gummere's.

ALTMAN, WALTER. "John Woolman's Reading." Unpublished Ph.D. dissertation, Florida State University. 1957.

BRAITHWAITE, WILLIAM C. *The Beginning of Quakerism.* Second Edition revised by Henry J. Cadbury. Cambridge: Cambridge University Press, 1955.

———. *The Second Period of Quakerism.* Second Edition prepared by Henry J. Cadbury. Cambridge: Cambridge University Press, 1961.

BRINTON, HOWARD (ed.). *Byways in Quaker History, A Collection of Historical Essays by Colleagues and Friends of William I. Hull.* Wallingford: Pendle Hill: Pendle Hill Pamphlets, 1944. Particularly germane to Woolman are the following essays: Rufus M. Jones, "Whittier's Fundamental Religious Faith"; Henry J. Cadbury, "Whittier as Historian of Quakerism"; D. Elton Trueblood, "The Career of Elias Hicks"; Thomas E. Drake, "Elihu Coleman, Quaker Anti-Slavery Leader"; Brand Blanshard, "Early Thought on the Inner Light"; H. H. Brinton, "Dreams of Quaker Journalists."

BRINTON, HOWARD. *Friends for 300 Years.* New York: Harper and Bros., 1952.

BROOKES, GEORGE S. *Friend Anthony Benezet.* Philadelphia: University of Pennsylvania Press, 1937. [See Chapter IV, n. 7, *supra.*]

DAVIDSON, ROBERT L. D. *War Comes to Quaker Pennsylvania, 1682–1756.* New York: Columbia University Press, 1957.

Drake, Thomas E. *Quakers and Slavery in America.*
New Haven: Yale University Press, 1950.

James, Sydney V. *A People Among Peoples: Quaker
Benevolence in Eighteenth-Century America.*
Cambridge: Harvard University Press, 1963.

Jones, Rufus M. *The Later Periods of Quakerism.*
2 vols. London: Macmillan and Co., 1921.

———. *The Quakers in the American Colonies.* London: Macmillan and Co., 1911.

Book IV herein is "The Early Quakers in New
Jersey" by Amelia Mott Gummere, and Book V
"The Quakers in Pennsylvania" by Isaac Sharp-
less. Mrs. Gummere's treatment of Woolman
prior to the intensive work on her major book
reflects the conventions of his nineteenth-cen-
tury reputation far more than her final portrait
of him. With the two volumes immediately pre-
ceding by Jones and the two books by William
Braithwaite (*supra*), this forms the grand set
of Quaker historical syntheses of the half century before our own generation of active re-
visionists.

———. *The Testimony of the Soul.* New York: The
Macmillan Co., 1937. Professor Jones, in the
full maturity of his years and powers, arguing
(with almost no reference to the unphilosophi-
cal Woolman) the intellectual grounds for taking the Woolman-like human phenomenon
seriously.

Kelly, Thomas R. *A Testament of Devotion.* New
York: Harper and Bros., 1941.

Another Quaker professor of philosophy works
his way as directly as he can into a renewal of
religious experience often specifically modeled
on Woolman's.

KRAUS, MICHAEL. *The Atlantic Civilization: Eighteenth-Century Origins.* Ithaca: Cornell University Press, 1949.

MASBACK, FREDERIC J. "The Economics of Evil: A Study of John Woolman's Thought." Pamphlet. Philadelphia: American Friends Service Committee, n.d.

PHILIPS, EDITH. *The Good Quaker in French Legend.* Philadelphia: University of Pennsylvania Press, 1932.

POMFRET, JOHN E. *The Province of West New Jersey, 1609–1702.* Princeton: Princeton University Press, 1956.

POWYS, LLEWELLYN. *Thirteen Worthies.* New York: American Library Service, 1923.

REYNOLDS, REGINALD. *The Wisdom of John Woolman.* London: G. Allen & Unwin, 1948.

SHORE, W. TEIGNMOUTH. *John Woolman: His Life & Our Times; Being a Study in Applied Christianity.* London: Macmillan and Co., Ltd., 1913.

THAYER, THEODORE. *Israel Pemberton, King of the Quakers.* Philadelphia: The Historical Society of Pennsylvania, 1943.

TOLLES, FREDERICK B. *James Logan and the Culture of Provincial America.* Boston: Little, Brown and Co., 1957.

——. *Meeting House and Counting House: The Quaker Merchants of Colonial Philadelphia, 1682–1763.* Chapel Hill: University of North Carolina Press, 1948.

TREVELYAN, GEORGE. *Clio, A Muse and Other Essays.* London: Longmans, Green and Co., 1913.

VINING, ELIZABETH GRAY. *Friend of Life. The Biography of Rufus M. Jones.* Philadelphia: J. B. Lippincott Co., 1958.

WHITNEY, JANET. *John Woolman, American Quaker*. Boston: Little, Brown, and Company, 1942. The definitive biography, with useful bibliography and appendices.

WOODWARD, CARL RAYMOND. *Ploughs and Politicks: Charles Read of New Jersey and His Notes on Agriculture, 1715–1774*. New Brunswick: Rutgers University Press, 1941.

WRIGHT, LUELLA M. *The Literary Life of the Early Friends, 1650–1725*. New York: Columbia University Press, 1932.

INDEX